The Look-It-Up Book of the
50 STATES

by Bill Gutman

illustrated by Anne Wertheim

Random House ⌂ New York

To the men and women who risk their lives for our freedom—B.G.

The author and editors would like to thank William L. Bird, Curator, Political History Collection, National Museum of American History, Smithsonian Institution, for his help in the preparation of this book.

Photographs: © AFP/CORBIS, p. 17; Photo courtesy of ARAMARK-Mesa Verde Co., p. 24; © Arkansas Department of Parks and Tourism/A. C. Haralson, p. 18; © Artemis Images, p. 47; © Brian Bahr/Allsport, p. 152; © Scott Barrow, Inc., pp. 66 (top), 95, 96; © Scott Barrow, Inc./SuperStock, p. 39; © Carolyn Bates, p. 140; © Tom Bean/CORBIS, p. 107; © Bettmann/CORBIS, pp. 9, 60 (bottom), 144; © Marcus Brooke/gettyimages, p. 92; © Kevin Burke/CORBIS, pp. 45, 90; © David Cannon/Allsport, p. 35; © Churchill Downs, Inc. and Kinetic Corporation, p. 57; © CORBIS, pp. 45, 51, 113; © Richard Cummins/CORBIS, p. 8; © Dan Curran/Dept. of Economic Development/Nebraska Division of Tourism, p. 86 (bottom); © Ron Dahlquist/SuperStock, p. 38; Photo courtesy Dartmouth College Library, p. 93; Courtesy Delaware Tourism Office, pp. 29, 30; © Jeremy D'Entremont, p. 62 (bottom); © 2000 Dodge City Convention & Visitors Bureau, p. 53; © Jack Dykinga/ gettyimages, p. 147 (left); © Melissa Farlow/gettyimages, p. 48; © David E. Fattaleh/West Virginia Division of Tourism, pp. 149, 150 (right); © 2001 The Flag Institute, pp. 4–5; © Kevin Fleming/CORBIS, p. 72; © Mark E. Gibson/CORBIS, p. 36; © Philip Gould/CORBIS, p. 86 (top); © David A. Harvey/gettyimages, p. 104; © R. B. Hayes Presidential Center/Courtesy of 1-800-BUCKEYE www.OhioTourism.com, p. 110; © Robert Holmes/CORBIS, p. 68 (bottom); Courtesy of Idaho Travel Council, pp. 41, 42; © Russell Illig/gettyimages, p. 116; © Iowa Department of Economic Development, Tourism Office, p. 50; © William Johnson/StockBoston, p. 68 (top); © Wolfgang Kaehler/CORBIS, p. 62 (top); Photo courtesy of Louisiana Office of Tourism, p. 59; © Mike Marsland/Yale University, p. 26; Minnesota Office of Tourism Photo, pp. 74, 75; © Mississippi Department of Economic and Community Development/Division of Tourism Development, pp. 77, 78; Photographs courtesy of Missouri Division of Tourism, p. 81; © David Muench/CORBIS, p. 15; Photo by Michael A. Murphy/TxDOT, p. 135; © Richard Murphy/*Anchorage Daily News*, p. 11; © Mystic Seaport, Mystic, CT, p. 27; © NASA, p. 33; © Nevada Commission on Tourism, p. 89; © New Mexico Department of Tourism, p. 98; © New Mexico Department of Tourism/Mark Nohl, p. 99; © North Dakota Tourism Division, p. 108; © Jack Novak/SuperStock, p. 120; © NPS, p. 56; © Oklahoma Tourism, p. 114; Photograph by Russell K. Pace, The Citadel, p. 126; © Pennsylvania Tourism, pp. 119, 120; © Tom Raymond/gettyimages, p. 131; Photo by Richard Reynolds/ TxDOT, p. 134; © Rhode Island Tourism Division, pp. 122, 123; © Royalty-Free/CORBIS, pp. 14, 20, 21, 63, 69, 80, 101, 102, 117, 120 (left), 128, 137, 143 (right), 146, 147 (right); © Harland Schuster, p. 54; © Dan Sears/UNC Chapel Hill, p. 105; © Donnie Sexton/Travel Montana/Courtesy of 1-800-VISIT-MT www.visitmt.com, p. 83; © Stephen J. Shaluta/West Virginia Division of Tourism, p. 150 (left); © Gail Shumway/gettyimages, p. 84; © Scott T. Smith/CORBIS, p. 138; © Joseph Sohm: ChromoSohm, Inc./CORBIS, p. 60 (top); © Joseph Sohm: Visions of America/CORBIS, p. 23; © SC Department of Parks, Recreation & Tourism, p. 125; Photo by South Dakota Tourism, p. 129; Photo courtesy of Tennessee, p. 132; © Roger Tidman/CORBIS, p. 32; Courtesy of Travel Michigan, p. 71; © Gary Vestal/gettyimages, p. 87; © Virginia Tourism Corporation, p. 143 (left); © VT Tourism & MKTG., p. 141; © 1998 Kennan Ward, p. 12; © Randy Wells/gettyimages, p. 44; © WI Dept. of Tourism/photo courtesy R. J. and Linda Miller, p. 153; © Mike Williams, ODNR/Courtesy of 1-800-BUCKEYE www.OhioTourism.com, p. 111; © Wyoming Travel & Tourism, pp. 155 (left), 156.

www.randomhouse.com/kids

Library of Congress Cataloging-in-Publication Data
Gutman, Bill. The look-it-up book of the 50 states / by Bill Gutman ; illustrated by Anne Wertheim.
  p. cm.
SUMMARY: Presents historical, geographical, and miscellaneous information about each of the fifty states.
Includes index.
ISBN 0-375-81213-X (trade pbk.) — ISBN 0-375-91213-4 (lib. bdg.)
1. U.S. states—Miscellanea—Juvenile literature. 2. United States—Miscellanea—Juvenile literature. [1. U.S. states. 2. United States—Miscellanea.]
I. Title: Look-it-up book of the 50 states. II. Wertheim, Anne, ill. III. Title.
E180 .G88 2002
973—dc21
2002020678

CONTENTS

Alabama · Alaska · Arizona · Arkansas · California

Hawaii · Idaho · Illinois · Indiana · Iowa

Kansas · Kentucky · Louisiana · Maine · Maryland

Massachusetts · Michigan · Minnesota · Mississippi · Missouri

Montana · Nebraska · Nevada · New Hampshire · New Jersey

    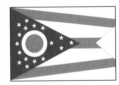

New Mexico · New York · North Carolina · North Dakota · Ohio

Oklahoma · Oregon · Pennsylvania · Rhode Island · South Carolina

South Dakota · Tennessee · Texas · Utah · Vermont

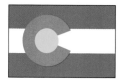
Colorado

Connecticut

Delaware

Florida

Georgia

INTRODUCTION

The United States of America is composed of fifty individual states. Forty-eight of the states are contiguous, or touching. They border each other and stretch from the Atlantic Ocean in the east to the Pacific Ocean in the west, from Canada in the north to Mexico in the south. The other two states are separated from the rest. Alaska is located at the northwestern corner of Canada, while Hawaii is a series of islands in the Pacific Ocean, approximately halfway between California and Japan. All the states but Hawaii are located on the continent of North America.

The differences between the states are often greater than the similarities. Whether it be climate, custom, geography, industry, population, or location, each state has a his-tory and tradition all its own. Life is very different in Maine than it is in Texas. In January, the weather in Bismarck, North Dakota, doesn't at all resemble the weather in Miami, Florida. The *United States* is truly an accurate and descriptive name. It is one country with its states united under a central government that represents all the people. At the same time, each state has an individual identity forged by its past and by its citizens.

Delaware was the first state in the Union, having voted to accept the Constitution of the United States on December 7, 1787. Arizona became the forty-eighth state on February 14, 1912. Alaska and Hawaii were granted statehood in 1959, completing the country as we know it today.

The Look-It-Up Book of the 50 States will introduce you to the individual states of the Union. It will describe how each became part of the United States, and how each continues to contribute to the country today. You'll also learn about places to visit, as well as resources contained within the boundary of each state. From tiny Rhode Island to mammoth Alaska, the United States is a mixture of many elements fused together to create a free and thriving country.

The author and editors fully acknowledge the positive contributions made by the District of Columbia and the U.S. territories of Puerto Rico, Guam, American Samoa, and the Virgin Islands. However, because this is specifically a book of the states, separate chapters on the territories have not been included.

Virginia

Washington

West Virginia

Wisconsin

Wyoming

State flower: Camellia

ALABAMA

State bird: Yellowhammer

With its humid, subtropical climate and short, relatively mild winters, Alabama is typical of a state in the Deep South. In fact, this state, located at the southern end of the Appalachian Mountains on the Gulf of Mexico, has often been called the Heart of Dixie. During its nearly 450 years of existence, the flags of Spain, France, Great Britain, and the Confederate States of America have flown over this southern land, giving it a diverse history.

Spanish explorers came to the area early in the sixteenth century, looking for gold. The Native American population decreased as the explorers spread European diseases and battled for land. The French were the first to successfully colonize the area in the mid-1600s. Black slaves were brought to the territory in 1719, and it was their hard labor that helped clear the land to raise food and pave the way for the products to be sold to support the colony.

At the beginning of the American Revolution (1775–83), all of Alabama north of West Florida was land reserved for Native Americans. After the Revolution ended, West Florida was returned to Spain and Alabama was turned over to the United States. Then, in 1813 and 1814, the U.S. government fought a series of battles against the Upper Creek Indians in Alabama. General Andrew Jackson led a force that won the decisive battle of Horseshoe Bend on the Tallapoosa River on March 27, 1814. On December 14,

1819, Alabama became the twenty-second state in the Union, with William Wyatt Bibb as its first governor.

Between 1820 and 1830, the population of Alabama doubled to over 300,000, and large cotton plantations were established. Caravans of additional slaves were brought in to work the fields. With cotton as its primary source of income, Alabama adopted the plantation system, which had been developed in Virginia and was organized around slave labor. Soon an elite group of wealthy planters dominated state society. This way of life would continue until the Civil War (1861–65).

In 1860, Alabama became the fourth state (after South Carolina, Mississippi, and Florida) to secede, or withdraw, from the Union. Montgomery became the first capital of the Confederacy, though the capital was shortly moved to Richmond, Virginia. After the Civil War ended in 1865, new railroads were built, which helped the state to industrialize.

The economy of the state began to change

around 1915, after the boll weevil—a beetle that infests cotton plants—so destroyed the cotton crop that farmers began raising livestock and looking to grow other crops.

During the 1950s and 1960s, Alabama was a focal point of the civil rights movement. It was one of a number of southern states practicing strict segregation, or separation of blacks and whites. The battle to desegregate often turned violent and was waged into the 1960s, when Governor George C. Wallace led the opposition to integrating the state's universities. That barrier fell when President John F. Kennedy called upon the National Guard to enforce the law of the land. Evidence that times had changed came in 1982, when George Wallace was elected governor for a fourth term. This time, Wallace was supported by black and white voters. Alabama was part of a new America.

Today, Alabama is the twenty-third most populous state in the Union. Birmingham is its largest city, followed by Mobile, Montgomery, and Huntsville. It is a beautiful state with many places of interest. In the north, reservoirs attract thousands of fishing enthusiasts each year. In the south, fishing and other water sports draw many visitors to areas along the Gulf of Mexico. There are four national forests as well as five state parks that welcome visitors year-round.

Another point of interest is the Tuskegee Institute National Historic Site, where visitors can tour some of the institute's original buildings as well as the home of Booker T. Washington, who founded the noted college for blacks in 1881. The Horseshoe Bend National Military Park contains the site where Andrew Jackson defeated the Upper Creek Indians in 1814. The U.S. Space and Rocket Center in Huntsville is another popular tourist attraction, as is Ivy Green, a cottage in Tuscumbia that was the birthplace and childhood home of famous author and lecturer Helen Keller. The World War II battleship *Alabama* is anchored in Mobile Bay and is open to tourists.

One of the rockets on display at the U.S. Space and Rocket Center in Huntsville, Alabama

Other Things to Know About Alabama

- Rickwood Caverns State Park, located north of Birmingham, is noted for its underground scenery. Within the caverns are limestone formations believed to be at least 260 million years old.
- Excavations at Russell Cave National Monument reveal that Native Americans dwelled in northeastern Alabama about 8,000 years ago. Other archaeological sites suggest that people lived in Alabama some 2,000 to 3,000 years before that.
- One of the landmark events in the struggle for civil rights took place in Montgomery in 1955, when an African American woman named Rosa Parks refused to give up her seat on a bus to a white person. Her subsequent arrest led to a peaceful boycott of buses in Montgomery, led by the Reverend Martin Luther King, Jr. The boycott ended in 1956, when the Supreme Court of the United States outlawed segregated public transportation.
- Alabama is the only state in the Union that has erected a monument to a bug. The Boll Weevil Monument in Enterprise commemorates the beetle that destroyed the 1910–15 cotton crops. That devastation forced farmers to begin growing other crops, thereby improving the economy and bringing more prosperity to the state.
- Much of the aeronautical research that enabled the United States to land the first person on the moon in 1969 was conducted at the George C. Marshall Space Flight Center in Huntsville.

NATURAL RESOURCES: wood, cotton, fish, peanuts, soybeans, coal, natural gas, sand and gravel, shale, stone, metal, and rubber

MANUFACTURED PRODUCTS: processed food, furniture and fixtures, chemicals, clothing, electronic equipment, rubber, plastics, textiles, transportation equipment, and metal, wood, and paper products

WILDLIFE: alligator, black bear, white-tailed deer, bald eagle, beaver, raccoon, opossum, weasel, otter, muskrat, poisonous and non-poisonous snakes, southern woodchuck, turtle, lizard, shrimp, tarpon, crab, and oyster

A SPORTS TRADITION

Sports have always had a great tradition in Alabama. The rivalry between the University of Alabama and Auburn University is one of the best-known in collegiate history. Famous Alabama sports personalities include Joe Namath, who played for Alabama's Crimson Tide, then later led the New York Jets to a Super Bowl triumph. Bo Jackson was a star running back at Auburn who went on to excel in both the National Football League and Major League Baseball, while Auburn basketball great Charles Barkley became a huge star in the National Basketball Association. Another native Alabaman was track star Jesse Owens, who won four gold medals at the 1936 Olympic Games in Berlin, Germany.

THE TUSKEGEE AIRMEN

On March 7, 1942, history was made when five African American men completed training and received their wings as fully trained fighter pilots and officers in the United States Army. It had taken a relentless effort during the early days of World War II to persuade the government to accept African Americans for flight training by the Air Corps.

A new aviation unit had been established near the Tuskegee Institute, where the pilots were trained. Eventually, a total of 926 pilots would graduate from the unit. They would fly 15,553 combat sorties, or missions, while fighting the Germans in North Africa and Italy. The pilots—part of the 477th Bombardment Group—established an unequaled record, not losing a single bomber to enemy aircraft.

ALASKA

State flower: Forget-me-not

State bird:
Willow ptarmigan
(TAR-mi-gun)

Alaska is America's last wilderness, the only place in the United States that can still be described as a frontier. While it is by far the largest state in the Union, it is also the most sparsely populated. In a way, Alaska remains an untamed and untapped land, full of natural resources—rivers, lakes, forests, mountains, glaciers, hot springs, and many species of wild animals. It features the highest mountain in North America and more lakes and rivers than any other state. Any way you look at it, Alaska is a wonderland.

There are four different climate zones in Alaska. Depending on the location, the average temperature ranges from moderate to bitterly cold. Some areas receive much rain; others get blowing snow and wind. The length of the day also varies. At Barrow on the Arctic coast, the sun is not seen from late November until late January. Yet in the summer at Barrow, there is continuous daylight from early May to early August.

There is still a kind of newness about Alaska. It has been a state only since 1959, and it became a United States territory only in 1867. The first inhabitants of Alaska were Siberian hunters from Russia who came over during the last ice age, 15,000 years ago. They were the forebears of the Inuit people, whose culture arose in Alaska some 4,000 years ago and who are thought to be the ancestors of present-day Native Americans.

Russia established the first permanent Alaskan settlement on Three Saints Bay in 1784. Though Russia had claimed the territory of Alaska as a colony, there was very little permanent settlement. At its peak, the Russian population numbered no more than 700. The United States—well aware of the active fur trade and Alaska's wealth of natural resources—had sent explorers there several times, but made no attempt to acquire the territory. Then, in 1867, the United States bought Alaska from Russia for $7.2 million, making it a U.S. territory. Secretary of State William Seward was responsible for getting the necessary votes in Congress to ratify the purchase. He felt Alaska's natural resources would be valuable to the United States in the future.

At first, many Americans thought buying the huge, untamed territory was a bad deal. They called it "Seward's Folly." But when gold was discovered in the Klondike region of

Canada in 1896, people changed their minds. By 1900, the town of Nome, Alaska, had become a tent city with more than 20,000 miners working claims. Another gold strike in the Tanana Valley of central Alaska led to the founding of the city of Fairbanks in 1902. The great Alaska gold rush was fully under way.

It was the gold rush that finally led to the growth and development of the territory. More people meant that more businesses were needed. Churches and schools were built. New towns sprang up almost overnight. Congress released funds for the U.S. Geological Survey to map and explore the territory more closely. Homestead laws were passed so that settlers could get title, or claim ownership, to land. Soon agricultural stations were set up to examine the suitability of the land for farming. The construction of the Alaskan Railroad began in 1915. The Alaska

Engineering Commission, in charge of railroad construction, set up headquarters in what soon became Anchorage. The commission installed water, electricity, sewage, and telephone facilities. Before long, there were schools and a hospital. Today, Anchorage is Alaska's largest city.

On January 3, 1959, President Dwight D. Eisenhower signed a proclamation admitting Alaska as the forty-ninth state of the Union.

At the start of the new millennium, the economy of Alaska has begun to change. Oil revenues, a staple for many years, are declining. The climate is not favorable to agriculture. Hunting and fishing are closely monitored, with restrictions and quotas on both industries. While there are huge coal reserves, only one coal mine is in operation in the state. Tourism, however, has increased every year since statehood.

THE IDITAROD

Alaska is the site of the most famous dogsled race in the world. The Iditarod is an annual 1,150-mile race from Anchorage to Nome. Though it was first held in 1973, it commemorates a historic event that took place in 1925. That year, a diphtheria epidemic threatened the city of Nome, and bad weather kept planes from delivering life-saving serum to its residents. So the serum was carried by dogsled teams, which raced the 674 miles from Nenana to Nome in 127.5 hours.

Despite its continuing problems, Alaska is still a land of beauty. Glacier Bay and Denali National Parks are major attractions. Many native Inuit live as their ancestors did hundreds of years ago, hunting whales and walruses. People still travel by dogsled. It is this mixture of the present and the past in America's last wilderness that makes Alaska such an intriguing state.

THE ALASKAN PIPELINE

The Alaskan pipeline carries oil from Prudhoe Bay on Alaska's remote northern coast to Valdez on its southern coast. It was constructed to help ease the energy crisis in the United States as well as to improve the economy of Alaska. The pipeline—which at the time was the most expensive private construction project ever undertaken—was completed in 1977. While it transported huge amounts of oil, it also led to one of the greatest ecological disasters in modern times. On March 24, 1989, the supertanker *Exxon Valdez* ran aground and dumped more than 11 million gallons of crude oil into Prince William Sound. It was the worst oil spill in North American history, doing enormous damage to the environment. The initial cleanup took three years, with a cost of more than $2.1 billion. The death toll in terms of wildlife was staggering, with the full impact still not completely known.

Other Things to Know About Alaska

- The only road into Alaska is the Alaska Highway. It was first built as a military supply route in 1942.
- The only World War II battle fought on North American soil began in Alaska on May 11, 1943, when U.S. troops drove the Japanese off the island of Attu in the Aleutians.
- The first Siberian hunters who came to Alaska actually *walked* there over the Bering Land Bridge. Eventually, as the ice age ended, the sea level rose to cover the bridge, and Alaska and Siberia were again separated by the Bering Sea.
- A cabbage grown during the Alaskan summer—when the sun might shine for twenty hours a day—can weigh up to eighty pounds!
- One of the greatest earthquakes of all time struck south central Alaska on March 27, 1964. It measured 9.2 on the Richter scale and within minutes caused more than $300 million in damage.

NATURAL RESOURCES: oil, natural gas, fish, wood, and fur

MANUFACTURED PRODUCTS: lumber, petroleum, wood and coal products, and rocket and payload products

WILDLIFE: bear (Kodiak, brown bear, black bear, grizzly bear, polar bear), deer, moose, mountain goat, fox, mink, wolf, coyote, otter, beaver, sea lion, harbor seal, sea otter, porpoise, whale, walrus, and caribou

State flower: Saguaro cactus blossom

ARIZONA

State bird: Cactus wren

The state of Arizona evokes many images of America's Old West. There are deserts, the magnificent Grand Canyon, tall cactus plants basking in the sun, and the legacy of the Apache Indian chiefs Cochise and Geronimo, as well as the frontier marshal Wyatt Earp. Arizona, however, has changed greatly since the nineteenth century, when it was a rough and dangerous territory dominated by miners and cattlemen, Indians and outlaws.

Today, the last of the lower forty-eight states (admitted to the Union on February 14, 1912) is a highly industrialized state complete with large, modern cities and farms and high-tech industries. At the same time, there is an incredible beauty to the landscape, while its climate is a mecca for tourists. The warm, dry Arizona air has always provided a healthy alternative for people with respiratory problems. Along with growth and industrialization, however, comes a modern problem—pollution. With a mixture of old and new, it's sometimes difficult to find a balance.

The Arizona landscape was formed over billions of years. The sixth largest state in the country is now 5,000 to 8,000 feet above sea level. Yet 2 billion years ago, scientists say, it was under a vast sea. Over the ages, the water receded, then rose, repeating the pattern over and over again. This phenomenon is what created Arizona's unique rock forma-

tions. Today, a semidesert region called the Colorado Plateau covers two-fifths of the state. Although the land was once totally under the sea, finding enough good water has always been a problem in modern Arizona.

Very few of Arizona's rivers flow steadily year-round. To compensate, eleven dams have been built to control the runoff from the Mogollon Rim, creating large artificial lakes. These lakes were created for flood control, irrigation, and hydroelectric power. The largest is Lake Mead, with an area of 233 square miles, formed behind Hoover Dam on the Colorado River. The magnificent dam, completed in 1936, has been a popular tourist attraction for many years.

Like many southern and western states, Arizona was already inhabited by Native Americans when it was first explored by the Spanish. As was the pattern, there were many battles between the two groups. By the

mid-eighteenth century, Spanish colonists were slowly moving into the area. The territory stayed under Spanish rule until 1824, when Mexico took control. Then, after the U.S.-Mexican War (1846–48), Arizona became a territory of the United States—and part of the American Wild West.

A war with the Apaches began around the time of the U.S. Civil War in 1861. Led by Cochise, the Apaches conducted raids against colonial settlements for nearly ten years. Finally, U.S. troops moved in to help. Cochise surrendered in 1871 and saw his people moved to a reservation. The Apache chief Geronimo continued to lead intermittent raids until September 1886, when he finally surrendered to General Nelson Miles.

At the same time, there was sporadic violence in the rugged cattle and mining towns. In 1879, the famed lawman Wyatt Earp settled in Tombstone with three of his brothers. They waged a constant battle against lawlessness. Gunfights were not uncommon. Eventually, however, the violence in the area began to subside.

After Arizona became the forty-eighth state of the Union in 1912, it began to grow and change along with the rest of the coun-

THE GRAND CANYON

The Grand Canyon is one of the natural wonders of the world. Located in the north-western corner of the state, it was slowly carved into the earth's surface by the Colorado River over many, many centuries. The canyon is 277 miles long and 18 miles wide, as well as more than 5,000 feet deep. Looking down into it from the rim, you can see massive rock formations stretching into the distance. They appear to vary in color, depending on the season and hour of the day. Designated a national park in 1919, the Grand Canyon now attracts some 5 million visitors a year, making it the most visited national park in the country.

try. More dams were built to help the farmers irrigate their land. Construction was started on a system of state highways. The days of the Wild West slowly faded into memory. Throughout it all, however, Arizona continued to have a large Native American population.

In 1948, the state's Native Americans won an Arizona Supreme Court case that gave them the right to vote in state elections. Then, in 1968, the first college on a Native American reservation opened its doors. It was the Navajo Community College in Tsaile. Today, Native Americans operate gambling casinos on their reservations to bring in money.

Arizona's two major cities are the state capital, Phoenix, with a population of more than one million, and Tucson, which is approaching 500,000. Phoenix is an administrative center, as well as the state's principal industrial and commercial city. Tucson is primarily a commercial and educational center, as well as a noted health and recreation resort.

Present-day Arizona is a thriving state. The University of Arizona and Arizona State University provide quality education and top-level collegiate sports programs. The Arizona Diamondbacks (baseball), Phoenix Suns (basketball), Arizona Cardinals (football), and Phoenix Coyotes (hockey) are professional sports teams that entertain fans and bring a sense of pride to the state.

Present-day Tombstone, Arizona

Other Things to Know About Arizona

- The northeastern corner of Arizona is the only place in the United States where four states meet. They are Arizona, New Mexico, Colorado, and Utah.
- The Petrified Forest National Park contains giant, ancient fallen trees that have slowly turned to stone over thousands of years.
- Phoenix is one major city winning the war on pollution. A 1993 survey showed that the amount of toxic chemicals discharged into the environment had been reduced by 34 percent from just four years earlier.
- By the mid-1990s, there were nearly 900,000 cattle and more than 160,000 sheep in Arizona.
- Oraibi—an Indian village on the Hopi reservation—has been constantly lived in for 800 years, longer than any other place in the United States.

NATURAL RESOURCES: beef cattle, sheep, vegetables, wheat, coal, copper, gemstones, sand and gravel, silver, gold, molybdenum, wood, stone, and clay

MANUFACTURED PRODUCTS: chemicals, processed food, transportation and industrial equipment, electronic equipment, heavy machinery, printed materials, scientific instruments, and wood, metal, stone, clay, and glass products

WILDLIFE: desert mule, peccary, horned lizard, rattlesnake, coral snake, desert tortoise, Gila monster, cottontail rabbit, pronghorn antelope, black bear, mountain lion, elk, bighorn sheep, golden eagle, hawk, and black vulture

GUNFIGHT AT THE O.K. CORRAL

The most famous gunfight in America's Wild West took place in Tombstone, Arizona, on October 26, 1881. That was when Marshal Wyatt Earp, his brothers Morgan and Virgil, and their friend John "Doc" Holliday shot it out with several suspected cattle rustlers at the O.K. Corral. In the gunfight, Tom and Frank McLaury and Billy Clanton were killed. All the facts regarding the event may never be known, but the gunfight has been depicted many times in Hollywood films. It is also reenacted on a regular basis for tourists who visit Tombstone, which is still preserved as a nineteenth-century ghost town.

State flower: Apple blossom

ARKANSAS

State bird: Mockingbird

Arkansas, the nation's twenty-fifth state, is often classified as one of the western south central states. While that description might sound confusing, a closer look shows that it fits Arkansas to a tee. The western, southern, and midwestern regions of the United States all seem to meet in Arkansas. Texas, which borders on the southwest, has always been considered part of America's Wild West. Missouri, which sits directly north of Arkansas, is part of America's heartland, or Midwestern states, while Louisiana and Mississippi, located south and southeast of Arkansas, have always been part of the American South.

In fact, various regions within Arkansas share the distinct feeling of their neighboring states. The southwestern section of the state, where grazing cattle compete for space among working oil fields, closely resembles the western plains. In the northwestern part of the state, dairy farms and orchards remind visitors of life in the Midwest, or Corn Belt. In the southeastern region, toward the Mississippi River, cotton plantations evoke the traditional Deep South.

Arkansas is a state that not only has gone through various periods and changes, but took a long time to adapt to the industrialized world of the twentieth century. Until the 1950s, Arkansas remained primarily an agricultural state, with farming the chief source of income. Unfortunately, there wasn't enough income to go around. The population of the state dropped as people left in search of a better livelihood. At that point,

industrialization began growing very rapidly. By the end of the 1950s, manufacturing had surpassed farming as the chief source of income. Soon the state would begin to live up to its nickname, the Land of Opportunity.

The Spaniard Hernando de Soto led the first European expedition through the southeastern United States, crossing the Mississippi in 1541 into what is today Arkansas. De Soto was looking for gold and silver, but found none; he died before the expedition ended. France was the next country to explore the new land, sending explorers down the river in 1673. Soon all the land west of the Mississippi River was claimed by France. After the area changed hands several times—going to Spain, then Great Britain, and finally back to France—the United States bought it as part of the Louisiana Purchase of 1803. By 1806, most of the present state was called the Arkansas District.

At first, settlers came slowly to the new territory. After 1817, however, the federal government began moving the Native American groups to new locations. Some traded their lands in Arkansas for new lands farther west. The Choctaw and Cherokee groups left the area in 1825 and 1828, respectively. Settlement increased rapidly. The population rose from just 14,000 in 1820 to more than 50,000 by 1835. A year later, Arkansas became the nation's twenty-fifth state, and the town of Little Rock, founded in 1821, became the state capital.

"Hard times" might be the best way to describe the early years of statehood. The state's two charter banks failed during the national depression of 1837, and it wasn't until the cotton boom of the 1850s that prosperity arrived. With prosperity, however, came increased slave labor, and when the Civil War broke out in 1861, Arkansas became the ninth state to secede from the Union. After the war, the state began rebuilding and the population grew, going from fewer than 500,000 people in 1870 to 1.3 million in 1900.

Farming was a difficult way of life in the early years of the twentieth century, especially for the sharecroppers and tenant farmers. If prices dropped, they were in danger of losing everything very quickly. Many had to deal with the threat of flooding from the Mississippi and Arkansas Rivers. The state has an abundance of water, all of it flowing southeastward to the Mississippi River, which forms Arkansas's eastern boundary. The Mississippi also winds its way across a wide flood plain. Despite the many rivers,

This house in Hope, Arkansas, is the birthplace of William Jefferson Clinton, the forty-second president of the United States.

there are no natural lakes in Arkansas. The largest bodies of water are reservoirs behind dams. The advent of the dams and other flood-control measures in the second half of the twentieth century has helped considerably.

Arkansas was in the national news in 1957, when the federal government ordered Little Rock's schools desegregated. Governor Orval E. Faubus then led a massive resistance that gained nationwide attention. But as in other southern states, the barriers of segregation eventually fell, and the state's politics became more mainstream. In 1978, Bill Clinton became governor, and fourteen years later he was elected president of the United States, serving two terms in office.

Today, Arkansas has a diverse economy, making it less susceptible to the agricultural disasters that crippled the state in years past. In fact, in the 1990s only about 6 percent of the workforce were employed in farming and agricultural services, forestry, or fishing.

While Arkansas remains one of the nation's leading cotton-producing states, industry is now the state's largest source of income.

Other Things to Know About Arkansas

- The name *Arkansas* is derived from a Quapaw Indian word meaning "south wind." The name was formerly spelled *Arkansa* and *Arkansaw*.
- Arkansas has the only diamond mine in the United States. Located in Pike County in the southwestern part of the state, the mine was worked from 1908 to 1925. In 1972, it became Crater of Diamonds State Park. Visitors are allowed to keep any diamonds they find.
- About half the land in Arkansas is covered with forest.

NATURAL RESOURCES: livestock, cotton, soybeans, rice, wood, natural gas, bromine, quartz, metal

MANUFACTURED PRODUCTS: processed food, furniture and fixtures, chemicals, electronic equipment, clothing, heavy machinery, plastics, and paper, wood, and metal products

WILDLIFE: black bear, deer, elk, bobcat, red and gray fox, poisonous and nonpoisonous snakes, largemouth and spotted bass, catfish, and alligator

Cathedral Room at Blanchard Springs Caverns

TOURISM AS AN INDUSTRY

Tourism provides an important source of income in Arkansas. Visitors to the state spend nearly $2.2 million each year, with almost 10 million people visiting the national and state parks. Among the points of interest in Arkansas are the Pea Ridge National Military Park (site of the Civil War battle at Pea Ridge), the Fort Smith National Historic Site at Fort Smith (where the first U.S. military post in the Louisiana Territory was established), and the Blanchard Springs Caverns near Mountain View (which contain miles of explored passages). There are five national parks, three national forests, and fifty-one state parks throughout Arkansas, as well as many annual events, ranging from the Arkansas Folk Festival in Mountain View to the World Championship Duck-Calling Contest in Stuttgart.

State flower: Golden poppy

CALIFORNIA

State bird: California valley quail

California might best be described as being as complex as it is large. Of all the states, it has the most people, the most automobiles, the most crops, the most construction and manufacturing, and the most students enrolled in colleges and universities. It also has the highest mountain peak outside Alaska in Mount Whitney, and features the lowest point in the country, a desert that is aptly named Death Valley. In addition, the state has a wide variety of weather conditions, a sometimes dangerous pollution problem, often too much or too little water, and fault lines with the potential to cause major earthquakes.

Nevertheless, people continue to flock to the Union's thirty-first state, which borders on the Pacific Ocean to the west and Mexico to the south, Oregon to the north, Nevada to the east, and Arizona to the southeast. The name *California* has been used in the region since 1542, when a Spanish expedition led by Juan Cabrillo came north from Mexico. It is thought the name was taken from a popular Spanish novel published in 1510 that had a fictional island paradise called California.

Cabrillo sailed into San Diego Bay and continued north along the coast. In 1579, the English explorer Sir Francis Drake sailed along the coast of northern California. Despite these two early expeditions, no Europeans would settle in California for nearly another 200 years. It was the Spanish who began settlements in the state in 1769. Most settlers were religious missionaries sent to try to convert Native Americans to

Christianity. Soon British, French, and American ships began trading with the Spanish coastal settlements. Four years after Mexico gained its independence from Spain in 1821, California became a Mexican territory.

By 1845, Mexico ruled huge areas of what is now the western and southwestern United States. The U.S. government wanted to purchase California and other parts of the Southwest, including the state of Texas. Mexico refused, and soon the two countries were at war. California was finally surrendered to the United States by the Treaty of Guadalupe Hidalgo on February 2, 1848, which formally ended the Mexican War. Some two and a half years later, on September 9, 1850, California became a state. Four years later, Sacramento became its permanent capital.

Economics most likely accelerated the

growth and quick conversion to statehood of California. On January 24, 1848, gold was discovered on the grounds of a sawmill on the South Fork of the American River, some thirty-five miles northeast of Sacramento. That started the greatest gold rush in United States history. Gold seekers, known as forty-niners, flocked to California from every part of the United States.

By 1852 (the year that gold production reached its peak), there were some 220,000 people in the state. Though the gold rush would end within two years, many of the prospectors stayed and became farmers and merchants. By 1855, the first state railroad line was completed, running twenty-two miles between Sacramento and Folsom. The first transcontinental railway was completed in 1869, with Sacramento the starting point from the west. In 1876, the line was extended south to Los Angeles.

California continued to grow rapidly at the beginning of the twentieth century. Between 1900 and 1930, the state's population increased from about 1.5 million to 5.7 million. Most of this growth was in the southern part of the state, around Los Angeles, where huge irrigation projects brought in water and allowed mechanized farming methods to thrive.

In April 1906, San Francisco was virtually destroyed by a huge earthquake—an event that would leave the entire state on alert from that point on.

In the latter part of the twentieth century, California experienced unprecedented

Sequoia National Park

NATIONAL PARK WONDERS

California's many national parks are among the most frequently visited in the country. Here are just a few of the most popular: Yosemite National Park is home to Yosemite Falls, the highest waterfall in North America. Sequoia National Park in central California has groves of giant sequoia trees—including one called the General Sherman, considered the most massive tree in the world. Redwood National Park in the northwestern part of the state has the tallest trees in the world, while Death Valley National Park (in both California and Nevada) is the largest national park outside Alaska. It contains the lowest land surface in the Western Hemisphere and the place where the highest temperature in the country has been recorded. All told, California's national parks have something for everyone.

growth. Freeways were built at an amazing rate, leading to massive traffic jams and air pollution. Airports, factories, and schools were also constructed, as the state became the most populated in the nation. Today, California is home to various ethnic and racial groups, sometimes leading to tension and urban violence. In addition to these man-made problems, California has had to deal with earthquakes, brush fires, mud slides, and drought in the closing decades of the twentieth century.

Yet California remains a land of beauty and wondrous extremes. There is snow in the northern mountains and a temperate climate at the shore in the south, which is also a region of very little rain. There are giant redwood trees in national parks, the legacy of the great Hollywood movie studios of the 1940s and 1950s, and an economy that continues to thrive. In the eyes of many, California is still a land of promise with the potential to grow . . . even more.

Golden Gate Bridge

Other Things to Know About California

- The world's tallest tree is a redwood in Humboldt County. It stands 365 feet tall and is 44 feet around.
- The oldest living things on earth are thought to be the bristlecone pine trees in California's Inyo National Forest—estimated to be over 4,700 years old.
- Lake Tahoe, sitting high in the Sierra Nevada Mountains on the California-Nevada state line, is one of the deepest lakes in the world.
- California is the most urbanized state in the country, with 93 percent of the people living in cities or towns.
- Professional sports teams abound in California. There are four Major League Baseball teams, three National Football League teams, four National Basketball Association teams, and three National Hockey League teams.
- Disneyland—the first major amusement park based on Walt Disney's classic cartoon characters—opened in Anaheim in 1955.

NATURAL RESOURCES: fruits and vegetables, milk, cattle, fish, oil, sand and gravel, limestone, and natural gas

MANUFACTURED PRODUCTS: aircraft and spacecraft parts, processed food, electronic components and accessories, cement, computers and computer software, and aerospace communications and guidance systems

WILDLIFE: black bear, mule deer, Roosevelt elk, bighorn sheep, red fox, cougar, bobcat, golden eagle, bald eagle, California condor, rattlesnake, Gila monster, gray whale, sea lion, sea otter, and elephant seal

---

EXECUTIVE ORDER 9066

During the nineteenth century, many Asians, including large numbers of Chinese and Japanese, immigrated to California in search of work. By the time World War II began, there were nearly 112,000 Japanese living in California, two-thirds of them U.S. citizens. Yet when Japan attacked Pearl Harbor on December 7, 1941 (thereby going to war with the United States), there was a tremendous distrust of Japanese Americans. On February 19, 1942, President Franklin Roosevelt signed Executive Order 9066, ordering that all people of Japanese descent be placed in internment camps for the remainder of the war. Many of these people lost businesses and homes, and even though they were allowed to return after the war, many decided to leave California and live elsewhere. It wasn't until 1988 that the United States government acknowledged the unfairness of this policy, when Congress passed a law to compensate those who had been interned.

COLORADO

State bird: Lark bunting

Though located in the western third of the United States, the eastern portion of Colorado is characterized by flat, treeless plains typical of the Midwest. The western part of the state, however, contains the Rocky Mountains, considered the traditional gateway to the West. And while Denver, the state's capital and largest city, is set on the plains just east of the Rockies, it is usually looked upon as a major city of the western United States. That's because a good deal of Colorado's history is steeped in what is commonly called the Old West.

The early history of the state is rife with Old West images of explorers, mountain men, trappers, and traders, as well as gold strikes, ghost towns, and friction with Native Americans. This was essentially a barren and dangerous territory before it was settled, and it wasn't tamed easily. In fact, Colorado's population didn't begin to grow significantly until the twentieth century had almost arrived.

Spanish explorers were the first Europeans to arrive in Colorado early in the eighteenth century. There were a number of Native American groups already there, including the Cheyenne, Arapaho, Kiowa, Comanche, and Ute. Yet that didn't stop Spain from claiming the entire region. Later in the century, the French would claim part of the territory as their own. When the United States bought the Louisiana Territory from France in 1803, there were questions about how much of Colorado belonged to France and how much to Spain. Zebulon Pike led the first U.S. expedition to Colorado in 1806, but the Spanish arrested him for crossing into their territory.

In 1819, Colorado was divided by treaty, with the southern and western part of the territory going to Spain, while the United States had the northern and eastern sections. Soon fur trappers entered the territory in search of beaver and other fur-bearing animals. Many trading posts were built, and the newcomers traded furs and manufactured goods with Native Americans. As trapping declined in the early 1840s, many of the trading posts were abandoned and many of the traders left.

After the U.S.-Mexican War (1846–48), all the former Mexican territories in North America were ceded to the United States, including the land of Colorado. Still, few people came to the new territory. Then, in 1858, gold was discovered in Cherry Creek in what is now downtown Denver. Mining camps sprang up as thousands of prospectors flocked to the area. Denver was built on lands previously reserved for the Cheyenne and Arapaho peoples. Having their land taken angered the Native Americans, and they began to raid the newly created stagecoach lines, making travel in the area increasingly dangerous.

The gold rush didn't last long, and when the Civil War (1861–65) left the territory without federal troops, there was virtually no defense against raids by Native Americans. At this point, the Cheyenne and Arapaho controlled most of the Colorado plains. Then, in November 1864, the U.S. Army returned to attack a village of sleeping Cheyenne and Arapaho at dawn. Two hundred men, women, and children were killed in what became known as the Sand Creek Massacre. By 1867, army troops had forced all the Native Americans, with the exception of the Southern Utes, off the Colorado plains and onto reservations in Oklahoma.

The battle for statehood began as the Civil War was winding down. One bill was stopped when Colorado voters rejected the proposed state constitution. A second try was vetoed by President Andrew Johnson because the territory wasn't populated enough. Finally, on August 1, 1876, Colorado became the Union's thirty-eighth state. The population increased from 40,000 in 1870 to more than 412,000 in 1890. At the same time, cattle ranching was becoming big business on the unsettled eastern plains. Thousands of farmers also began settling in the new state after irrigation to dry areas was started in 1870. Between 1870 and 1880, silver was discovered in several mountain locations.

Gold was discovered at Cripple Creek in 1891, keeping the mining industry profitable until it was stalled by serious labor problems in the first decades of the twentieth century. In the 1920s, oil production increased, further boosting the economy and attracting more workers. The state's population rose over the one million mark for the first time in 1930.

Following World War II (1939–45), there was yet another population boom, centered mostly around Denver. Rural areas of the state actually lost people. Industry continued to change, and Colorado's economy today depends more on tourism, service industries, and other small industries such as scientific research and high-technology development. Skiing, in particular, has become a huge industry. Old mining towns like Aspen are now luxurious ski resorts. In other areas, new

The twin peaks of Maroon Bells are perhaps Colorado's most recognizable feature.

towns such as Vail were created for the sole purpose of skiing.

Today, Colorado is a mixture of old and new. Deserted ghost towns in the mountains are offset by crowded vacation destinations, and pollution is a problem in some areas. All of this can make it hard to believe that Colorado once lacked enough people to be considered for statehood.

LABOR-MANAGEMENT CONFLICT LEADS TO VIOLENCE

In the late nineteenth and early twentieth centuries, mining played a large role in Colorado's economy. However, it was just the owners of the mines who were getting rich. The miners themselves felt they weren't being paid enough for their hard and sometimes dangerous labor. The first strike occurred in Leadville in 1880, when miners were told they could not talk on the job. There was another strike at Cripple Creek in 1893, when owners tried to increase the workday from eight to ten hours. But the worst strike occurred near Ludlow in 1913 and 1914 at coal mines owned by John D. Rockefeller. The strikers—many Greek and Slavic immigrants—built a tent settlement after they were evicted from company-owned housing. On April 20, 1914, National Guard troops tried to clear the camp. The miners resisted, and thirty-nine people were killed in the gun battle. The two sides fought for ten days, until President Woodrow Wilson sent federal troops in to restore peace.

Other Things to Know About Colorado

- The suspension bridge over the Royal Gorge of the Arkansas River in Colorado is the highest such bridge in the world, at 1,053 feet above ground.
- In 1893, Katharine Lee Bates went up Pikes Peak in the Rocky Mountains in a horse-drawn carriage. She took a good look from the top, came down, and wrote the song "America the Beautiful."
- The name *Colorado* comes from the Spanish word meaning "reddish." It was first given to the Colorado River because of its reddish color.
- The United States Air Force Academy is located on a beautiful campus near Colorado Springs.

NATURAL RESOURCES: beef and dairy cattle, sheep, wheat, vegetables, corn, coal, wood, gold, lead, natural gas, petroleum, sand and gravel, silver, stone, uranium, and zinc

MANUFACTURED PRODUCTS: processed food, electronic and transportation equipment, heavy machinery, chemicals, clothing, printing and publishing, scientific instruments, rubber, plastics, and wood, glass, stone, and clay products

WILDLIFE: bison, pronghorn elk, prairie dog, coyote, black bear, moose, red and gray fox, bobcat, beaver, mule deer, bighorn sheep, mountain lion, golden eagle, and western rattlesnake

PREHISTORIC COLORADO

There is evidence that people lived in what is now Colorado long before recorded history. Tools and campsites found by archaeologists in eastern Colorado suggest that humans lived there as early as 10,000 B.C. The first people known to have settled in what is now southwestern Colorado were the Anasazi, who apparently came to the area about 1500 B.C. The Anasazi and their descendants lived in Colorado until nearly A.D. 1300. Many built houses of stone and adobe (sun-dried brick) along the canyon walls below the overhanging rims of the mesas. These people became known as Cliff Dwellers. Toward the end of the thirteenth century, a changing climate, decreasing natural resources, and a severe drought forced the Anasazi to move. It would be several hundred more years before Colorado's recorded history began.

State flower: Mountain laurel

CONNECTICUT

State bird: Robin

One of the six so-called New England states, Connecticut is located in the northeastern United States, the section where the country was first colonized by the British. It is the fifth of the original thirteen states, having ratified the Constitution of the United States on January 9, 1788. Connecticut is also the third smallest state in the Union, and in many ways still reminds people of its colonial roots.

One of the earliest of the industrialized states, Connecticut supplied the needs of the early colonists, as well as the tools of battle from the American Revolution (1775–83) through World War II (1939–45). Only then did the economy begin to change. Today, Connecticut is mainly an urban and sub-urban residential state. It has few of the open spaces of the larger states of the American South and Southwest. It also has a large commercial presence, with many major corporations choosing to move out of New York City to the suburbs. The state remains in the forefront of the nation's business machinery.

It was a very different world when the first settlers came to Connecticut. The Dutch were the first to arrive after an exploration in 1614. By the early 1630s, the fertile river valley section of the area began to attract settlers from the Plymouth and Massachusetts Bay Colonies in

Massachusetts. Before that time, the area was inhabited solely by Native Americans. There were several groups, all of whom spoke Algonquian languages. They lived by hunting deer, catching fish, and growing corn, beans, and squash. They moved from the forested lands to the coastal areas during different seasons of the year.

In the latter sixteenth century, it is thought that an epidemic greatly reduced the number of Native Americans in the area. For the most part, the new settlers and Native Americans got along well, trading goods and living in relative peace. By about 1640, the English settlers from Massachusetts greatly outnumbered the Dutch.

There was one war—a conflict in 1637 between settlers and the Pequot tribe. With the help of both the Mohegan and the Narraganset to the east, the colonists launched a major attack on a Pequot village at Mystic River. The defeat was so devastating to the Pequot that the few who survived scattered into distant territories or were sold into slavery. In January 1639, the colony of Connecticut was officially formed, and the colonists wrote a set of laws known as the Fundamental Orders, which significantly advanced democratic government.

The colonists living in Connecticut played a large role in events leading up to the American Revolution, with representatives at the First Continental Congress in 1774. Though there were no major battles on Connecticut soil, troops from the area fought in all other battles. Three heroes of the Revolution—Ethan Allen, Israel Putnam, and Nathan Hale—were from Connecticut, as was Benedict Arnold, perhaps the most famous traitor in American history.

After the Revolution, Connecticut remained at the forefront of an increasingly industrialized nation. Eli Whitney began manufacturing cotton gins in New Haven in 1793. The machine revolutionized the cotton economy of the South. In 1839, Charles Goodyear of Naugatuck invented the process to vulcanize rubber, making it stronger, more elastic, and resistant to temperature change. By the end of the nineteenth century, Connecticut was known for Colt and Winchester firearms, International silverware, Seth Thomas clocks, Hitchcock chairs, Stanley tools, Royal typewriters, and a wide variety of precision metal tools.

During both world wars, the state was a major manufacturer of munitions and military products. World War II saw Connecticut produce Pratt and Whitney airplane engines, Hamilton Standard propellers, Cheney silk parachutes, and Electric Boat submarines. After the war, Connecticut became the first producer of nuclear-powered submarines and a major supplier of Sikorsky military helicopters.

Through the 1980s—as more corporations began setting up headquarters in major cities—Connecticut became mostly a middle-class, suburban state. But the larger cities such as Hartford, New Haven, Waterbury, Bridgeport, and Stamford had to deal with the problem of impoverished minority communities and an increasing crime rate. This is a problem that continues

Yale University in New Haven

today, a situation many states will have to deal with in the twenty-first century.

From New Haven to rural pockets in the northwestern corner of the state, Connecticut continues to be an interesting and diversified place. It has always played a major role in America's development.

NATIVE AMERICAN ECONOMICS

As with almost all other states, Native Americans inhabited Connecticut before European settlers arrived. And, as in other states, it was the Native Americans who ultimately lost their lands and sometimes their culture and heritage. Beginning in the 1980s, descendants of Native Americans began seeking to regain ancient lands and also to find ways to improve their economic conditions. One group of surviving Pequot—the Mashantucket Pequots of Ledyard, whose ancestors had fought against settlers in Connecticut—not only settled a land claim, but in 1992 opened a gambling casino on their reservation in 1992. Today, the Foxwoods casino is a major attraction in Connecticut as well as a big money-maker. The success of the Pequot paved the way for similar ventures in Connecticut and in other states as well.

AMERICA'S HISTORY ON DISPLAY

As one of the original thirteen states, Connecticut has a history that mirrors much of the rest of early America's. There are many historical sites in the Constitution State to see and enjoy. Among them: the Webb House at the Webb-Deane-Stevens Museum in Wethersfield, where George Washington met with French officers during the American Revolution to plan the Yorktown campaign; the Revolutionary War Office at Lebanon, where Governor Jonathan Trumbull conferred with Washington, Benjamin Franklin, the Marquis de Lafayette, and other leaders; and Mystic Seaport, in Mystic, a restored village that features a street of early nineteenth-century vintage, as well as the last of the old-time whaling ships. That's just a start.

Other Things to Know About Connecticut

- The nation's first library for children opened in Salisbury in 1803.
- It was Roger Sherman of Connecticut who settled a debate at the Constitutional Convention by dividing Congress into two separate houses. The Senate would have two representatives from each state, while the House would have varied numbers of representatives from each state, depending on that state's population.
- The first woman to receive an American patent was Mary Kies of South Killingly. In 1809, she was given a patent for inventing a machine to weave straw with silk or thread.
- The USS *Nautilus*—the world's first nuclear-powered submarine—is on permanent display at the shipyard at Groton.
- The name *Connecticut* is thought to have been derived from an Algonquin word, *Quinnehtukqut,* meaning "beside the long tidal river."

NATURAL RESOURCES: fish and shellfish, dairy products, eggs, vegetables, tobacco, clay, sand and gravel, and stone

MANUFACTURED PRODUCTS: aircraft parts, helicopters, industrial machinery, electronic equipment, metal products, printed materials, transportation equipment, submarines, jet aircraft engines, and ball bearings and roller bearings

WILDLIFE: white-tailed deer, red fox, coyote, bobcat, black bear, beaver, raccoon, cottontail rabbit, bald eagle, ruffed grouse, ring-necked pheasant, great blue heron, wild turkey, striped bass, flounder, bluefish, perch, pickerel, and brook trout

Mystic Seaport

State flower: Peach blossom

DELAWARE

State bird: Blue hen chicken

Although Delaware is the second smallest of the states in area, it will always be remembered as the first state to ratify the Constitution of the United States, back when the nation was new. Occupying part of the peninsula between Delaware Bay and Chesapeake Bay, Delaware was one of the thirteen original states and one of the earliest to be settled in the New World.

Despite these historical beginnings, Delaware has often been a center of controversy. From the time it was first settled, there have always been various groups within the state wanting very different things. Even today, there are two distinctly different regions within the state, which is almost bisected by the Chesapeake and Delaware Canal.

North of the canal, the state is densely populated and highly industrialized. South of the canal is a much more rural, lightly populated region that continues to be largely agricultural. Ironically, the state's name is derived from that of the governor of another state. In 1610, Captain Samuel Argall, who was sailing for Virginia, sighted what is now known as Cape Henlopen in Delaware Bay. Argall, however, named it Cape De La Warr, in honor of Thomas West, Third Baron De La Warr, who was Virginia's first colonial governor.

English explorer Henry Hudson is thought to have discovered the Delaware Bay in 1609, while he was employed by the Dutch East India Company. More Dutch ships explored the Delaware River between 1614 and 1620. Four years later, the Dutch West India Company claimed the land from the Delaware Valley to the Hudson River Valley with the hope of colonizing the area. But colonization didn't happen until 1631, when the Dutch set up the first European settlement in Delaware on the site of present-day Lewes. Within a year, however, everyone living there was killed by Native Americans. That would be the only attack of its kind on European settlers in Delaware.

In the following years, the English and Dutch began competing for land in the Delaware Valley. There were several small wars for the territory. The English finally took possession after a treaty between the two countries in 1674. In December 1682, the three Delaware counties were united with Pennsylvania. The area still didn't have its

WINTERTHUR

The Henry Francis du Pont Winterthur Museum, Garden, and Library, in Winterthur, has exhibits of furniture and household goods from 1640 to 1840, which give visitors a glimpse of life in early Delaware.

own identity. It wasn't until 1704 that the three counties of Delaware became a separate colony.

After the Revolutionary War (1775–83), Delaware's John Dickinson became instrumental in framing the Constitution of the United States. The Delaware state convention quickly voted to adopt it, becoming the first state to do so in 1787. By 1790, the state had a population of 59,096, including almost 4,000 free blacks and 9,000 black slaves. The state was already becoming industrialized in the Wilmington area to the north. In 1795, Delaware's first cotton mill was opened, and in 1802, the firm of E. I. du Pont de Nemours & Company opened. The company would supply nearly all the military explosives used by the United States, and would become one of the world's largest chemical manufacturing firms. It remains based in Delaware to this day.

During the Civil War (1861–65), Delaware was considered a border state, with many Confederate sympathizers. But the state remained part of the Union. Though it had economic ties with the South, in 1860 there were fewer than 2,000 slaves among the

almost 22,000 blacks living in the state. More than 13,000 Delawareans served in the Union Army; yet even after the war ended, the state usually aligned itself with the southern bloc of the Democratic Party.

It wasn't until the industrial boom of World War I (1914–18) that the Wilmington area really began growing. By 1920, the state's urban population exceeded its rural

THE FIRST FAMILY OF DELAWARE

When French immigrant Eleuthère Irénée du Pont de Nemours established a gunpowder mill near Wilmington in 1802, no one could have known what that would eventually mean to the entire state. The Du Pont family continued to run the company through the years, until it evolved into one of the world's largest chemical manufacturing firms. In addition to boosting Delaware's economy, the family has contributed to the state in many philanthropic ways. They built modern schools and highways throughout the state, and promoted the creation of the state's first "welfare home." The Du Ponts have done more than earn money for themselves. They have given back to the state they have always called home.

population for the first time. During World War II (1939–45), newfound industrial capabilities allowed Delaware to produce ships, airplanes, motor vehicles, iron and steel, chemicals, foodstuffs, and additional goods to help the war effort. Both agriculture and industry prospered.

During the 1950s, Delaware was one of the fastest growing states on the eastern seaboard. Yet its public schools remained segregated, much like those of the Deep South, until the Supreme Court ruling of 1954. Segregated housing was also in evidence throughout the state until federal legislation was passed to end it in 1968. There were economic problems in the 1970s and early 1980s.

The economy began reversing itself in the later 1980s, when relaxed regulations on interest rates attracted more than a dozen out-of-state banks to locate their credit card operations within the state. More banks came in the 1990s, spurring a construction boom. Delaware today is the corporate home of hundreds of major and minor corporations.

It seems that the First State has always battled for its own identity. Though problems remain, the Delaware of the twenty-first century is definitely moving in the right direction.

ONLY ONE TIME

In contrast to other areas, the relationships between European settlers and Native Americans in Delaware was almost always friendly. There was, however, one violent encounter in the very early days of settlement. It happened in 1631, when a group of Dutch merchants built Swanendael, the first European settlement in Delaware, on the site that is now Lewes. Within a year, the settlement was destroyed and the settlers killed by Native Americans. It was the only attack ever made on European settlers in Delaware. The reason for the attack—and the identity of the Native American group that was involved—remains uncertain to this day.

Other Things to Know About Delaware

- Wilmington is the only large city in Delaware, yet its population is well under 100,000. Dover, the next largest city, barely has 30,000 residents.
- The white-tailed deer is the only large game animal found in Delaware today.
- Early settlers in Delaware came from Sweden, Finland, the Netherlands, France, and England, making the territory an early example of the melting pot that was to become America.

NATURAL RESOURCES: corn, chickens, eggs, soybeans, fruits and vegetables, sand and gravel, and magnesium compounds

MANUFACTURED PRODUCTS: electric and electronic equipment, chemicals, paper products, processed food, instruments, paint and varnish, dyes, cloth and cloth finishes, synthetic fibers, and paper, rubber, and plastic products

WILDLIFE: white-tailed deer, fox, raccoon, mink, otter, beaver, great blue heron, black duck, snapping turtle, copperhead snake, crab, clam, and a variety of small birds and fish

Delaware had the first log cabins built in America. One that was built in 1638 can still be seen at Fort Christina State Park in Wilmington.

State flower: Orange blossom

FLORIDA

State bird: Mockingbird

No one knows if Juan Ponce de Leon was really looking for a fountain of youth when he first explored Florida in 1513, but the Sunshine State has become at least a figurative fountain for the thousands of retired Americans who now go there to live. Florida's growth has been astounding. Between 1950 and 1970, Florida's population grew by amazing 145 percent. Then, between 1970 and 1980, it increased by another 43.4 percent. By 1990, the population had jumped 32.7 percent more!

With more than 14.5 million residents, Florida today is the fourth most populated state in the Union. The huge increase was mainly due to people moving there from other places. With its temperate climate, Florida is a haven for retirees who no longer want to deal with cold, snowy winters. It has also become a haven for refugees from Cuba, an island located off Florida's southernmost tip. So Florida today is a melting pot, with many problems associated with large populations and industrial growth.

How different it must have been when Juan Ponce de Leon first set foot on Florida soil in 1513. It was this Spanish explorer who named the state, calling it *La Florida*, which translates roughly as "land of the flowers." It is estimated that there were some 350,000 Native Americans living there when Ponce de Leon first arrived.

As more explorers came, the number of Native Americans fell dramatically. They had no resistance to European diseases such as measles, smallpox, and typhoid fever. By the mid-eighteenth century, they were wiped out. In 1565, a Spanish colony was established at San Agustin, now Saint Augustine. That was the first permanent settlement in what is now the United States. By the early seventeenth century, England and France were contesting Spain's claim to the vast Florida area. English settlers began pushing southward from New England. After the French and Indian War (1754–63), Spain gave the British Florida through treaty. But following the American Revolution (1775–83), the British returned the territory to Spain. Finally, in 1821, the United States completed a treaty with Spain that formally gave the U.S. permanent possession of Florida.

Life in the area began to quickly change.

Florida drafted a state constitution in 1838 and, on March 3, 1845, became the Union's twenty-seventh state. Population growth began almost immediately. Between 1845 and 1860, the number of Floridians increased from about 70,000 to more than 140,000, with most of the people living in the northern part of the state. At that time, huge tracts of land in the southern part of the state were uninhabited. But plantations in central Florida were already producing large crops of cotton using slave labor. Lumber, leather, salt, and coarse cotton cloth also contributed to the early economy.

Florida was one of the Confederate states to secede from the Union during the Civil War (1861–65). Like most white people of the other southern states, many Floridians didn't want their way of life to change. After the war, however, slavery was abolished, and, in 1868, Florida was readmitted to the Union. In the years after the war, Florida, like other states in the Deep South, became segregated. Whites continued to find ways to keep blacks in an inferior position, a situation that would remain for nearly another century.

Land development began in the late nineteenth century. At the same time, the southern part of the state began to grow. Citrus growers were forced to move farther south when several severe winters damaged the crop in the north. During World War I (1914–18), Florida's resort business blossomed because travel to foreign lands was restricted. In the early 1920s, nearly one million tourists a year began going south to Florida. Speculators saw the potential, and the real estate boom began. Between 1920 and 1925, Florida's population increased four times faster than that of any other state.

Soon the Miami area in the south was being developed. Swamps and mudflats were drained, forests cleared, and roads and railroads extended southward. The first real estate boom ended in 1926, but it began again after World War II (1939–45). Over the next thirty years, the face of the state changed. Cities grew, hotels and resorts sprang up, retirement communities were built for senior citizens. Attractions such as Disney World were opened, and professional sports teams established franchises in all the major sports.

WATER, WATER, EVERYWHERE

Florida is surrounded by water on three sides, and has the longest coastline of all the states except Alaska. But that isn't the only water in this low-lying state. Besides a number of rivers, Florida has more than 7,000 lakes greater than ten acres in size. The state is also noted for its springs, many of which bubble up from underground reservoirs. A number of these springs turn into swift streams called runs. Some of the larger springs pour out more than 500 million gallons of water a day. There is no shortage of water in the state, so long as it can be kept clean.

White ibis

Everglades National Park is one of the largest swamps in the world, with many species of wildlife.

Florida today is trying to solve the problems of a still increasing population and changing demographics. Services for seniors are constantly in demand; tourists and college students continue to flock to the state; and the number of new immigrants from Cuba and other Latin American countries is increasing. Crime is on the rise, as is pollution resulting from overpopulation.

The warm climate of the Sunshine State, which has always been so attractive to so many people, may prove to be its biggest challenge yet.

Other Things to Know About Florida

- The oldest existing masonry fort in the United States lies within Castillo De San Marcos National Monument in Saint Augustine.
- Marineland of Florida, on the coast between Saint Augustine and Daytona Beach, is the world's first oceanarium, housing many interesting species of marine life.
- Andrew Jackson, who would become the seventh president of the United States, was once the military governor of Florida.
- One of every five people in Florida is over the age of sixty-five.

NATURAL RESOURCES: citrus fruits, vegetables, beef cattle, honey, milk, sugarcane, limestone, natural gas, peat, petroleum, phosphates, titanium, and fish

MANUFACTURED PRODUCTS: chemicals, electronic and transportation equipment, instruments, processed food, printed materials, and wood products

WILDLIFE: alligator, Florida panther, black bear, white-tailed deer, Key deer, wild pig, manatee, poisonous snakes, marine turtles, land turtles, and numerous species of fish and birds

WATCH THE WEATHER

Because of its location at the southernmost point in the United States, Florida is vulnerable to severe weather patterns coming out of the tropics, most notably hurricanes. Over the years, a number of major hurricanes have devastated the state. Two disastrous hurricanes, in 1926 and 1928, temporarily derailed Florida's first real estate boom. In August 1992, southern Florida was hit by Hurricane Andrew, the costliest natural disaster in U.S. history. The storm killed forty-one people and left more than 200,000 homeless. Property damage was estimated to be about $20 billion. When meteorologists predict the approach of bad weather, Floridians must pay careful attention.

The first U.S. space satellite, *Explorer I,* and the first manned spacecraft, *Apollo II,* were both launched from Cape Canaveral, home of the Kennedy Space Center.

Launch of the space shuttle *Atlantis,* from the Kennedy Space Center in 2000

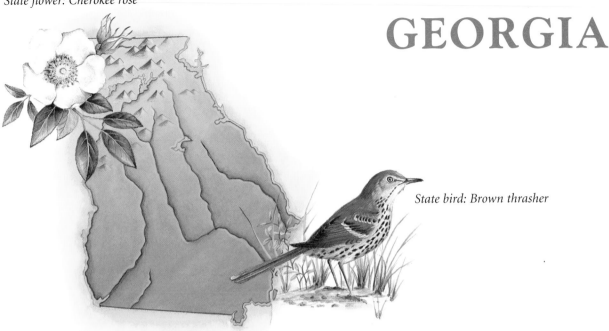

State flower: Cherokee rose

GEORGIA

State bird: Brown thrasher

The fourth state to enter the Union and one of America's thirteen original colonies, Georgia has a long and checkered history. Prior to the Civil War (1861–65), the state typified the lifestyle and economic prosperity that was the Old South. After the Civil War, it became one of the poorest states in the union. Today, however, Georgia is a benchmark for the New South, with its capital, Atlanta, an important economic center for both the South and the entire nation.

To say that Georgia has come a long way is an understatement. The first explorers found a state almost entirely blanketed by forest. In fact, Georgia today still has more woods per square mile than any other state. Yet from this once dense foliage, great plantations arose. Later, after the flames of the Civil War had seemingly destroyed the state, a new Georgia was built. A state that was once filled with slaves and then made segregation a policy well into the twentieth century, Georgia also produced the likes of baseball great Jackie Robinson, the first African American to play in the major leagues; and Civil Rights movement leader Martin Luther King, Jr., as well as cable television news pioneer Ted Turner.

Spanish explorer Hernando de Soto was the first European to come into the area after landing in Florida in 1539. In 1566, Pedro Menéndez de Avilés founded a mission and fort on Saint Catherines Island. During the next 100 years, the Spanish built similar forts and missions along the state's entire coast. They called the area *Guale*. During this period, the English also made a claim on the area.

After the English founded a colony at Charleston (now South Carolina) in 1670, the settlers began pushing southward. Soon battles broke out, and by 1686, the English had forced the Spanish from the entire territory. Then, in 1732, King George II of England granted a charter for a colony to be called Georgia. The king wanted a buffer colony to protect the Carolinas from the Spanish in Florida. It was an odd beginning.

After the American Revolution (1775–83), Georgia became the fourth state to ratify the new Constitution, and the first southern state to do so. Growth began almost immediately, with the population rising from around 83,000 in 1790 to 252,000 in 1810. When gold was discovered in the northern part of the state in 1828, even more people came. This caused most of the remaining Native Americans to move from, or be driven out of, the territory.

At the same time, Georgia was building an agricultural economy based on slave labor. In 1860, four of every nine persons in the state were slaves. That didn't mean all free whites in Georgia kept slaves. It was estimated that one-tenth of the people held nine-tenths of the wealth. Georgia was already one of the richest states in the nation. The Civil War (1861–65) would change all that. Georgia voted to secede in January and joined the Confederate States of America.

During the war, Georgia was a major supplier of food and arms to the Confederate Army, but before the war ended, the state would pay a bitter price. In 1864, the Union Army, led by General William Tecumseh Sherman, invaded Georgia. That September, Sherman and his men burned Atlanta, then marched to the sea, looting homes, destroying bridges, railroads, factories, mills, and warehouses. Finally, in December, Sherman and his army captured Savannah. When the war ended, slavery had been abolished, but a once wealthy state was in ruins.

It wasn't easy to rebuild. The large plantations were broken up into smaller farms operated by tenant farmers and sharecroppers. There was little cash available. Farming would not be profitable again until after World War II (1939–45). There was some profit after World War I (1914–18) and into the 1920s, but soon the boll weevil destroyed much of the cotton crop, and thousands began abandoning their farms and going to the cities. From the end of the Civil War to the middle of the twentieth century, Georgia was one of the poorest states in the Union. In 1940, the average Georgia family earned only 57 percent as much as the typical family nationwide.

Change came again during World War II. Bell Aircraft built a plant in Marietta, and turned it from a sleepy town into a booming industrial center. Bell would close after the war, but it reopened in 1950 as the Lockheed Corporation, continuing as a major employer with many government contracts. Soon more national corporations began to move south, especially to the capital of Atlanta.

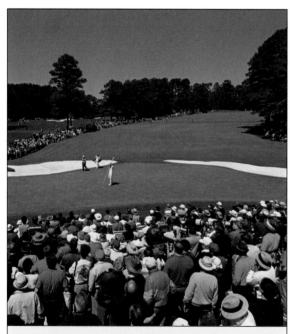

The U.S. Masters Golf Championship is played each year in Augusta, Georgia.

CABLE NEWS PIONEER

When Ohio-born Ted Turner inherited his father's small outdoor advertising company at the age of twenty-four, no one could realize what he would eventually build. He used the profits from the ad company to buy an Atlanta UHF television station (TBS) in 1970. Just a decade later, he would again use his profits to start an all-news cable TV network. The result was Cable News Network, or CNN—the first all-news station of its kind. Turner went on to establish a communications empire. He became owner of the Atlanta Braves baseball team, and even won the America's Cup sailing trophy for the United States. But it was CNN that carried Atlanta's name across the seas and attracted a number of foreign companies to the area, helping to revitalize the state's economy.

More old barriers fell when Jimmy Carter became governor in 1971 and promptly announced, "I say to you quite frankly that the time for racial discrimination is over." Carter called for equal opportunity for all, and five years later was elected the first Georgian president of the United States. Soon most vestiges of the old ways began to disappear. Toward the end of the century, Georgia was growing more rapidly than the nation as a whole.

Georgia's population in 1996 was at more than 7.35 million, making it the tenth most populated state in the country. Although the state was once losing population, more people are now moving into Georgia than leaving. There is still work to be done, but the state has overcome several periods of bad times to become a progressive part of a new century.

Atlanta played host to the Summer Olympic Games in 1996. The Olympic rings fountain commemorates this.

THE TRAIL OF TEARS

The Cherokee Nation of north Georgia was the last group of Native Americans left in Georgia. They prospered by adopting many ways of white settlers. In 1821, a Cherokee scholar named Sequoya invented an alphabet for writing the Cherokee language. Soon after, the nation adopted a constitution that created a democratic government. They also started a newspaper, the *Cherokee Phoenix*, published in both Cherokee and English. The nation prospered. Some wealthy Cherokee even began using slaves in their fields. But with the discovery of gold on Cherokee land in 1828, life changed quickly. Whites rushed to Georgia to find the precious metal. In 1832, the state held a lottery distributing Cherokee lands among whites. Finally, in 1835, a treaty was produced ordering the Cherokee to move west. Federal troops were sent in to make sure the order was followed. About a quarter of the Cherokee Nation died in stockades or during the forced march west. The march became known as the Trail of Tears.

Other Things to Know About Georgia

- An Atlanta drugstore was the first place to serve Coca-Cola, in 1887.
- The first radio station owned and operated by African Americans started in Atlanta in 1949.
- The first steamship to cross the Atlantic, the *Savannah*, sailed from the city of the same name in 1819.
- Georgia is the largest state east of the Mississippi River.
- The Andersonville National Historic Site, in west central Georgia, commemorates the thousands of Union soldiers who were imprisoned and died at the infamous Andersonville prison during the Civil War.

NATURAL RESOURCES: peanuts, pecans, cotton, beef cattle, chickens, eggs, soybeans, peaches, sweet potatoes, sand and gravel, stone, marble, granite, and lumber

MANUFACTURED PRODUCTS: chemicals, electronic equipment, transportation equipment, clothing, printed materials, textiles, and rubber, plastic, wood, paper, and glass products

WILDLIFE: alligator, white-tailed deer, black bear, bobcat, red fox, gray fox, beaver, hawk, black vulture, turkey vulture, poisonous and non-poisonous snakes, and various fish and shellfish

HAWAII

State bird: Hawaiian goose

The fiftieth state of the Union is unique in many ways. Not only is Hawaii made up of a series of eight main islands, it is located in the Pacific Ocean, some 2,400 miles from the West Coast of the United States. According to historians, the islands have only been inhabited for about 1,000 years, so they do not have as much ancient history as most areas on the mainland. Images of Hawaii vary from that of a vacation paradise with glorious beaches and hula dancers to that of the Pearl Harbor Naval Base, where Japanese planes attacked on December 7, 1941, plunging the United States into World War II (1939–45).

Hawaii is actually an island chain that extends for about 1,600 miles, between the island of Hawaii in the southeast and Kure Island in the northwest. Scientists believe that the chain of islands has been forming for many millions of years because of volcanic activity on the ocean floor. Today, there is a single active volcano on the island of Maui, and there are three on the island of Hawaii. Hawaii is almost twice the size of the other islands combined.

It is thought that the first inhabitants of Hawaii probably came from two island groups in the eastern part of Polynesia—the Society Islands, which include Tahiti; and the Marquesas Islands. These early settlers probably migrated to Hawaii between the seventh and thirteenth centuries. To get there, they would have had to travel more than 2,000 miles in long, catamaran-like canoes.

By the time the first Europeans arrived in the late eighteenth century, there were an estimated 300,000 native inhabitants. They relied on fishing, farming, and the gathering of wild plants for food. With no metal or metalworking skills, they made weapons, household utensils, and tools from wood, stone, shell, and bone.

The first westerner to arrive in Hawaii was the British explorer Captain James Cook, in 1778. Cook reached the islands of Oahu, Kauai, and Niihau. Later that year, he returned to explore Hawaii and the other islands. He originally named the chain the Sandwich Islands in honor of a British nobleman, the Earl of Sandwich. While relations between the native Hawaiians and Cook's men were initially good, bad feelings soon arose over the theft of a boat. In 1779, there was a violent encounter between the two groups, and Cook was killed.

From about 1785, however, the islands

Kilauea Volcanoes National Park on the Big Island of Hawaii

became an increasingly important provision port for European and North American ships trading with East Asia. Some ships stayed for several months, and the crewmen began to mingle with the native Hawaiians. By 1820, a small number of these foreigners had settled permanently in the islands. The newcomers introduced cattle, horses, and orange trees, as well as other plants and domestic animals, to the islands. Unfortunately, they also introduced a number of infectious diseases. With no immunity, many Hawaiians died. The population dropped from 300,000 at the time of Cook's arrival to about 135,000 in 1820.

In the early nineteenth century, Hawaii was a kingdom governed by a king. But the islands' first written constitution in 1839 began giving more rights to the common people. The first trade treaty with the United States became effective in 1876, and in 1887, when the treaty was renewed, the United States also gained exclusive rights to the use of Pearl Harbor, on Oahu. By 1894, a constitutional convention was convened, the result being the end of the monarchy. Hawaii was now a republic. Finally, on June 14, 1900, Hawaii officially became a U.S. territory, making all its people citizens of the United States.

By 1940, the population had reached about 423,000, due mostly to immigration. There had also been an expansion of U.S. military facilities, bringing many more U.S. soldiers and sailors to Pearl Harbor. That set the stage for the surprise Japanese attack on December 7, 1941, which plunged the United States into war. Because of its strategic location, Hawaii was the principal staging area for U.S. operations in the Pacific. Pearl Harbor was a major repair base for damaged warships, and thousands of mainland civilians moved to Hawaii to work.

After the war, life changed rapidly. Between 1950 and 1960, the population jumped from approximately 500,00 to 633,000. At the same time, Hawaii began developing a large-scale tourist industry and a more diverse manufacturing sector that included cement plants and food processing. That wasn't all. Efforts to make Hawaii a state were also intensified, and on August 21, 1959, the islands became the fiftieth state of the Union.

Hawaii is now a thriving state, a fabulous vacationland, and a place of uncompromising beauty. Its peoples represent something unique as well: a fusion of races that more or less makes all Hawaiians part of so-called minority groups. Because of this, there is little racial discrimination. Hawaiians live in a harmonious combination of different races, languages, religions, and cultures.

Other Things to Know About Hawaii

- Hawaii's Mauna Loa is the largest active volcano on earth.
- Mount Waialeale on Kauai is the wettest place in the world, with a 460-inch average annual rainfall.
- The Hawaiian Islands once produced more than 40 percent of the world's supply of canned pineapple and more than 70 percent of its pineapple juice.
- Hawaii has had only a few short railroads. They were built before World War II to carry sugar and pineapples, and to move military supplies. Today, only one tourist line on Maui still remains.
- Hiram L. Fong, a Chinese American living in Hawaii, became the first person of Asian ancestry to be elected to the U.S. Senate.
- Hawaiian-born Duke Paoa Kahanamoku represented the United States in four Olympic Games, beginning in 1912. He was one of the world's great swimmers, winning three gold medals and two silvers. He later appeared in several Hollywood films.

NATURAL RESOURCES: sugarcane, pineapples, vegetables, coffee, melons, milk, flowers and nursery products, sand and gravel, stone, pumice, and shrimp

MANUFACTURED PRODUCTS: clothing, processed food, glass products, and printing and publishing

WILDLIFE: a wide variety of birds and fish. The only native mammal is a rare insectivorous bat. All other mammals, such as dogs, pigs, cattle, sheep, goats, cats, and axis deer, were introduced by settlers, who also introduced reptiles and amphibians such as frogs, toads, turtles, lizards, geckos, and a blind, burrowing snake.

SWEET AS SUGAR

The most important crop in Hawaii is sugarcane. In the early 1990s, Hawaii's average annual raw sugar production exceeded 600,000 metric tons. That represents about one-fifth of the raw sugar produced from sugarcane in the United States. Sugar has been part of the Hawaiian economy for a long time. The decline of the whaling industry in the 1860s, created a need for a new source of revenue. A treaty with the United States in 1876 to provide the sugar duty-free spurred the growth of the industry. American investors saw the potential, and by 1890, the islands supplied about 10 percent of the raw sugar refined each year in the United States.

Traditional Hawaiian hula dancer

State flower: Idaho syringa

IDAHO

State bird: Mountain bluebird

With its unique location in the northwestern part of the country, Idaho borders on six other states as well as Canada. To the west are Washington and Oregon, to the south sit Nevada and Utah, while both Montana and Wyoming share Idaho's eastern border. A narrow strip of land, known as the Panhandle, extends all the way to the Canadian border, and gives the state its unique shape.

Known as the Potato State, Idaho once produced 27 billion potatoes in a single year, which breaks down to 120 potatoes for every man, woman, and child in the United States. Much of Idaho is covered by the Rocky Mountains, with wide expanses of plateaus and upland slopes, giving the state some of the finest forest lands in the United States. It is sparsely populated. Only the fortieth most populated state (with just over one million residents), Idaho is the fourteenth largest state in area. It was also the last of the fifty states to be explored by white men.

Though there is evidence of prehistoric migratory hunters living in the territory more than 12,000 years ago, there were just seven Native American groups living in what would become Idaho in 1805. That was when an expedition led by Meriwether Lewis and William Clark entered the territory. They were sent by President Thomas Jefferson to seek a water route to the Pacific Ocean.

When word about the heavily forested territory got out, fur traders began coming into the area. In 1809, a Canadian company founded the first trading post in the entire Idaho, Washington, and Oregon area.

By 1825, more traders and mountain men were arriving and exchanging goods with Native Americans. Additional trading posts and forts were built. In fact, there was so much trapping and trading that by the early 1840s, the fur traders had greatly reduced the region's fur supply. That left just two trading posts in operation: Fort Hall and Fort Boise. Both would later become outposts on the Oregon Trail.

In 1846, the area called the Oregon country (which included the Idaho region) became a U.S. territory. The region would be redefined several more times until the final boundaries of Oregon, Washington, Idaho, Montana, and Wyoming were set. That didn't happen until 1868, when Boise became the capital of the Idaho Territory. Eight years earlier, gold had been discovered in the section of Idaho that was occupied by the Nez Perce people.

Because of the find, thousands of miners flocked to camps above the Clearwater and Salmon Rivers and in the mountain basin north of present-day Boise. Though the gold rush lasted only a few years, the influx of people would serve as a base group for the first permanent settlement in the interior of the Pacific Northwest. Another consequence of the gold rush was that, once again, Native Americans in the area were forced to move from their traditional lands onto reservations.

Cattle were first introduced to Idaho from California and Texas in the 1860s, to supply mining communities. It wasn't long, however, before Idaho's fine grazing lands began attracting cattle ranchers and sheepherders. By the 1880s, sheep and cattle raising had spread across much of the area. Once the railroads came in—starting in 1874—the area developed quickly. The population grew from 33,000 in 1880 to 89,000 in 1890.

On July 3, 1890, Idaho became the forty-third state to join the Union. The new state made more progress shortly after the turn of the century, when the Carey Land Act of 1894 finally resulted in major irrigation projects in Idaho. One such project resulted in the building of the Arrowrock Dam on the Boise River in 1915. It was the highest dam in the world at the time.

The state's economy received another boost during World War II (1939–45), when its natural resources—including timber—were needed for a variety of military purposes. Silver and lead were used in weapons, and farms provided large amounts of food staples. After the war, the lumber industry continued to grow and flourish.

By the 1970s, despite a still relatively small population, Idaho began experiencing some modern problems. Under the guidance of Governor Cecil Andrus, legislation was passed to conserve the state's forests, rivers, and streams. People came to hike and fish, and enjoy the beautiful outdoor setting. Tourism began to grow as older industries, such as logging and mining, declined.

Today, much of Idaho remains as it was when Lewis and Clark arrived nearly 200 years ago—a mountainous, forested land with the look of an unspoiled country. It still holds a small part of America's wilderness between its borders.

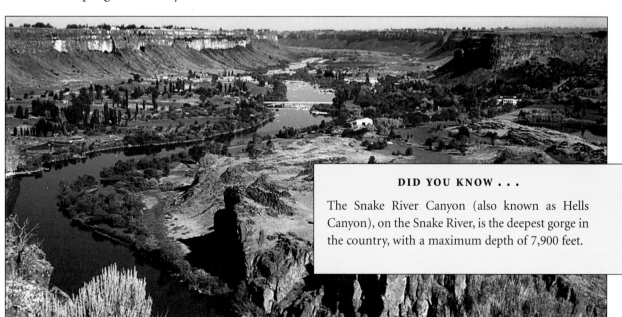

DID YOU KNOW . . .

The Snake River Canyon (also known as Hells Canyon), on the Snake River, is the deepest gorge in the country, with a maximum depth of 7,900 feet.

THE NEZ PERCE WAR

In June 1877, the Nez Perce were told to leave their fertile homelands in northeastern Oregon. They resisted, and federal troops were sent in. Led by Chief Joseph, the Nez Perce fought off the troops and began a long march toward the safety of the Montana-Canada border. The U.S. Army, under General O. O. Howard, pursued them. Chief Joseph waged a brilliant campaign, but in October, after traveling some 2,000 miles across the roughest terrain in the West, he surrendered. In his message to General Howard, he said, "Hear me, my chiefs, my heart is sick and sad. From where the sun now stands I will fight no more forever."

Potato field

Two-thirds of all potatoes in the United States are grown in Idaho.

IDAHO'S NATURAL WONDERS

Idaho's unspoiled wilderness contains a number of natural wonders that often leave visitors in amazement. Thousand Springs is a group of natural springs that cascade from canyon walls along the Snake River. Shoshone Falls, also on the Snake River, are higher than Niagara Falls and drop 212 feet over a horseshoe-shaped rim. Another tourist attraction is Balanced Rock, southwest of Buhl. It is a massive rock whose bottom part has been worn away by wind erosion through the ages. The rock, which is 40 feet high, appears precariously balanced on a base that is only 3 feet wide.

Balanced Rock

Other Things to Know About Idaho

• The first hydroelectric power plant built by the federal government was the Minidoka Dam on the Snake River in Idaho. Work began on the plant in 1909.
• Two out of every three farms in Idaho rely on artificial irrigation for their water supply. Considering there are more than 20,000 farms in the state, that represents a considerable irrigation effort.
• A disastrous forest fire in northern Idaho and adjoining Montana in 1910 scorched one-sixth of Idaho's northern forests, greatly slowing the increasingly profitable lumber industry.

NATURAL RESOURCES: potatoes, hay, wheat, beef cattle, sheep, milk, lumber, barley, garnets, gold, lead, molybdenum, sand and gravel, and silver

MANUFACTURED PRODUCTS: food products, chemicals, electric and electronic equipment, machinery, wood and paper products, and printed materials

WILDLIFE: moose, antelope, woodland caribou, elk, cougar, grizzly bear, black bear, mule deer, white-tailed deer, bighorn sheep, mountain goat, coyote, red fox, wolverine, otter, whistling swan, bald eagle, golden eagle, marsh hawk, osprey, salmon, trout, largemouth bass, and sturgeon

ILLINOIS

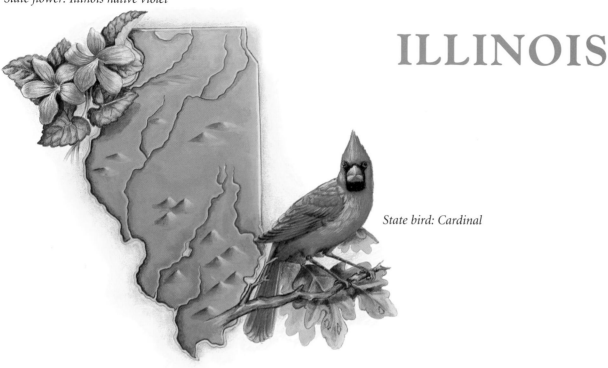

State bird: Cardinal

A famous song lyric rhapsodizes: "My kind of town, Chicago is . . . my kind of town." As the third largest city in America, Chicago is the kind of town millions can enjoy, as well as being the centerpiece of the state of Illinois. With the Mississippi River as its western border and a short stretch of Lake Michigan on the northeast, Illinois is in the heart of the American Midwest, an area of flat or gently rolling plains that was once covered by prairie grasses. From that land configuration, Illinois acquired the nickname The Prairie State.

Others prefer to call it the Land of Lincoln. That's because former president Abraham Lincoln lived in the state capital of Springfield for seventeen years. But then again, Illinois is known for many different things—from the Chicago stockyards to the rolling plains of corn to the ultrabusy O'Hare Airport. The state also has a colorful history, including the famous Chicago fire of 1871 and the infamous Al Capone (and other high-profile gangsters) of the Roaring Twenties. Though Illinois is just twenty-fifth in size among the fifty states, it ranks sixth in total population. It has its finger on the pulse of much of what is happening in the entire country.

The first European explorers to come to the Illinois country, as it was already called, were Frenchmen Louis Jolliet and Jacques Marquette. They traveled down the Mississippi River along the western boundary of the present state in 1673. Other Frenchmen came soon after and began building forts and missions along the Mississippi. The town of Cahokia on the Mississippi, the first permanent settlement in the Illinois country, was founded as a French mission in 1699.

More French settlers began to arrive, trading with Native Americans, farming the fertile valleys, and raising livestock. Before long, the British began coming as well. At first, both groups got along with each other, as well as with the Native Americans already living there. Toward midcentury, however, a series of wars between the three groups began, culminating with the French and Indian War (1754–63), which ended with the Treaty of Paris in 1763. Under the terms of the treaty, the French ceded the Louisiana

Territory east of the Mississippi, which included Illinois, to Great Britain.

After the American Revolution (1775–83), Britain surrendered the territory that included Illinois to the United States, and in 1787 it became part of the larger Northwest Territory. A short time after Illinois became the nation's twenty-first state, on December 3, 1818, present-day boundaries were finally set. In 1837, a blacksmith named John Deere developed a new, all-steel plow that turned the prairie soil much more effectively. That—and other improved farm equipment—enabled the farming industry in the area to boom.

While no battles were fought on Illinois soil during the Civil War (1861–65), more than 250,000 of its citizens served in the Union Army, including General Ulysses S. Grant. On February 1, 1865, with the end of the war in sight, Illinois became the first state to ratify the Thirteenth Amendment to the Constitution of the United States, which abolished slavery.

Increasing industrialization in the late nineteenth century led to a period of labor-management conflict, as Illinois had many

Sears Tower

44

miners and factory and railroad workers. There were disputes over wages, hours, and working conditions. Several of the strikes turned violent before they were settled. In the early years of the twentieth century, Illinois was in the forefront of the labor movement. It was the first state to establish an eight-hour workday and to limit children to working forty-eight hours of work each week. At the same time, Illinois was one of the three leading manufacturing states in the country.

When the stock market crashed in October 1929, Illinois joined the rest of the nation in a decade-long depression. The farming industry probably suffered the most. The massive effort needed during World War II revived statewide industry and boosted farm production. Yet in the 1960s and 1970s, there were both population and economic declines, because many of the old plants and factories had become inefficient.

New technology and the influx of foreign companies helped spur the economy in the 1980s and 1990s. Manufacturing now gener-

The Lincoln Home National Historic Site in Springfield features the only home Abraham Lincoln ever owned. It contains many pieces of furniture owned at one time by the Lincoln family.

ates fifteen times the income that agriculture does, yet Illinois still ranks as one of the most productive farming states in the nation. In fact, only Iowa produces more corn than the Prairie State. Illinois is also second in raising hogs, and large numbers of cattle are shipped to Illinois for fattening from ranches in the western states.

Chicago remains a vibrant city. O'Hare is the world's busiest airport, while the Sears Tower is the tallest building in North America. More than 2.8 million people live in the Windy City. By contrast, the second largest city is Rockford, with just about 150,000 residents. While Chicago is the hub, the rest of Illinois has a strong identity as well.

Other Things to Know About Illinois

- The world's first skyscraper, the ten-story Home Insurance Building, was completed in Chicago in 1885.
- Illinois has more miles of public highways and roads than any single state, other than Texas and California.
- The first radio station in Illinois was WDZ, which began broadcasting at Tuscola in 1921; it has since moved to Decatur.
- Chicago's professional sports teams have always had loyal followings. The Bears in football, and the Cubs and White Sox in baseball, go back to the early years of the twentieth century. In the 1990s, basketball's Chicago Bulls won six championships in eight years, led by the legendary Michael Jordan.
- The famous historical debates between Abraham Lincoln and Stephen A. Douglas took place at seven locations in Illinois in 1858.

NATURAL RESOURCES: corn, hay, soybeans, fruits and vegetables, hogs, beef cattle, milk, coal, petroleum, sand and gravel, and stone

MANUFACTURED PRODUCTS: machinery, chemicals, electric and electronic equipment, processed food, metals and metal products, printed materials, and transportation equipment

WILDLIFE: bison, elk, black bear, muskrat, mink, weasel, white-tailed deer, beaver, coyote, Canada goose, and bald eagle

State flower: Peony

INDIANA

State bird: Cardinal

Bordered by Ohio, Kentucky, Michigan, and Illinois, Indiana is considered part of America's Midwest. It is one of the leading industrial and agricultural states in the country, as well as a state where sport is king. Basketball is revered everywhere, the Indianapolis 500 auto race is legendary, and Notre Dame football has had Indiana on the map since the days of coach Knute Rockne in the 1920s.

The name *Indiana* literally means "land of the Indians," yet there are virtually no Native Americans remaining in the state. Its nickname—The Hoosier State—also presents a puzzle. While people living in Indiana are often called "Hoosiers," no one seems able to agree on the origin of the word. All of this combines to make the state an interesting place with its own unique history.

The French were the first Europeans to explore the region in 1679. By 1710, French traders were exchanging wares with many of the twelve Native American groups that inhabited the area. Some of these groups were also new to the territory, having moved west as settlers encroached on their traditional lands to the east. After 1715, the French began building a chain of military posts designed to prevent British fur traders from entering the territory.

Great Britain, however, took over all for-mer French land claims east of the Mississippi, including the Indiana region, following the end of the French and Indian War (1754–63). The first permanent settlers were inhabitants of the thirteen American colonies to the east, who had decided to look for a better life in the west. After the American Revolution (1775–83), present-day Indiana was incorporated into the Northwest Territory; then, in 1800, it was renamed the Indiana Territory. The Indiana Territory included present-day Indiana, as well as all of Michigan, Wisconsin, Illinois, and parts of Minnesota. The huge area was still sparsely populated, with only about 5,600 settlers living there.

When Indiana became our nineteenth state on December 11, 1816, its present-day boundaries were finally set. There were a few more battles, but by 1838 most Native Americans were forced to leave and settlers began arriving faster. In 1860, there were approximately 1.35 million residents in Indiana. At that time, the principal source of revenue was farming. Industry began developing after the coming of the railroads in the 1840s and 1850s.

Indiana fought on the Union side in the Civil War (1861–65). There were several battles fought on Indiana soil before Confederate troops were driven out. Industrial growth began almost immediately after the war. Factories were built to meet a growing demand for manufactured goods, and, at the same time, coal mining became a major industry. In 1886, natural gas was discovered in east central Indiana, spurring a flurry of growth in that region.

Labor-management conflict in the latter part of the century resulted in many workers joining unions such as the Knights of Labor, the American Federation of Labor, the United Mine Workers of America, and the American Railway Union. All this activity led to the passage of more progressive labor laws, enabling Indiana to avoid much of the violence that was prevalent in other parts of the country in the late nineteenth century.

At the start of the twentieth century, there was another wave of industrial growth that, by 1920, had transformed Indiana into a prominently urban, industrial state. In the northwest, there was a focus on heavy industry. United States Steel located its Midwestern mills in Calumet in 1905. The need for workers attracted many immigrants from southern and eastern Europe, and by 1920, the state had a population of almost 3 million.

The Depression years of the 1930s were tough for those living in Indiana, as they were for much of the country. But after World War II (1939–45) ended, the economy, which had grown during the war years when its factories churned out tanks, airplanes, and communications equipment, continued to surge. Another major change occurred in 1949, when Indiana's schools were desegregated by law.

In 1967, the city of Gary—which in 1965

THE INDY 500

The Indianapolis 500 is the most famous auto race in the world. It was first held in 1911 and is run annually at the Indianapolis Motor Speedway on the Sunday of Memorial Day weekend in May. Each year, thirty-three drivers qualify to compete in the 200-lap race around a 2.5-mile oval-shaped race course. Three drivers have won the race four times. They are A. J. Foyt, Al Unser, and Rick Mears. The fastest Indy 500 was run in 1990, when Dutch driver Arie Luyendyk completed the race at an average speed of 185.981 miles per hour.

The Speedway's nickname is The Old Brickyard. That's because the track's surface was paved with 3.2 million bricks in late 1909. Though the surface is now made of asphalt, the nickname has stuck. Each year, the Indy 500 is attended by more than 350,000 spectators.

had become only the second U.S. city after Washington, D.C., to have a majority population of African Americans—elected Richard Hatcher to be one of the first African American mayors of a major city.

During the early 1990s, Indiana's service industries were growing, and the pharmaceutical and agricultural chemical industries expanded. The state also overtook Pennsylvania as the nation's leading steel producer. Plans for two additional automobile manufacturing plants were announced in 1995. Redevelopment also continued in downtown Indianapolis, where a $300 million Circle Centre Mall covered more than ten city blocks.

Though no one knows the exact origin of the name Hoosier, the Hoosier State continues to grow, prosper, and make major contributions to the country at large.

Corn farmer

Other Things to Know About Indiana

- New Harmony, Indiana, was the first place in the United States where boys and girls were taught in the same classes.
- Ice sheets once covered nearly all of Indiana. The ice sheets left a deep layer of glacial drift that weathered into soil made up of sand and clay, mixed with gravel.
- There are still more than thirty covered bridges in Parke County alone.
- Hall of Famer Larry Bird—one of the greatest basketball players of all time—was born in Indiana and grew up in the town of French Lick.
- Many majestic animals once roamed the Indiana territory, but disappeared by the time of rapid settlement in the early nineteenth century. They include the bison, or American buffalo, the black bear, wildcat, and timber wolf.
- The Lincoln Boyhood National Memorial, alongside the large Lincoln State Park in Spencer Country, includes the site of the cabin where Abraham Lincoln lived between the ages of seven and twenty-one, and also the grave of his mother, Nancy Hanks Lincoln.

NATURAL RESOURCES: corn, soybeans, coal, hay, clay, gypsum, stone, peat, petroleum, sand and gravel, and iron

MANUFACTURED PRODUCTS: steel, transportation equipment, electronic equipment, industrial machinery, chemicals, and metal, rubber, and plastic products

WILDLIFE: red fox, white-tailed deer, muskrat, mink, raccoon, woodchuck, migratory birds, ring-necked pheasant, prairie chicken, turkey vulture, hawks, and owls

THE VISION OF TECUMSEH

As settlers headed west in the seventeenth and eighteenth centuries, Native Americans were slowly driven from their traditional lands, at first moving west, then finally confined to reservations. Like many other Native American chiefs, the Shawnee Tecumseh didn't want to see his people pushed out of the land they knew as home. Tecumseh felt the only chance his people had was to forget intertribal rivalries and band together. In 1811, Tecumseh headed southward to carry his message of confederation to the Chickasaw, Choctaw, and Creek peoples. He told his brother, known as the Shawnee Prophet, not to attack federal troops, which were near the Prophet's Town. Ignoring Tecumseh's orders, the Prophet ordered an attack. The Battle of Tippecanoe followed, and while it wasn't a decisive victory for the Americans, the town was destroyed and the spirit of the Native American confederation broken. Tecumseh's vision of uniting his people to stop the Americans from taking their land fell far short of its goal.

State flower: Wild rose

IOWA

State bird: Eastern goldfinch

Iowa has been described as a large-scale production line for the nation's food. Almost all of the state's history revolves around farming. Overall, Iowa is the nation's third most productive agricultural state, behind only the much larger California and Texas. In the mid-1990s, there were some 100,000 farms in Iowa, with about three-quarters of the land devoted to crops, the rest being mostly pasture. Iowa ranks first in the production of corn and second, after Illinois, in the production of soybeans. The Hawkeye State, as Iowa is called, also ranks third in the value of livestock and livestock products, and is among the leading milk-producing states in the country.

Located west of Illinois and east of Nebraska, Iowa is in the heart of the Midwest, the nation's Corn Belt. Even though industrialization has grown to a large extent in recent years, the majority of Iowa's industrial output is based on farm production.

Iowa's mainly flat land area was formed tens of thousands of years ago by glaciers. It is thought that ice once covered much of the state. Ice sheets moving over the land wore away at existing hills and filled in valleys, giving the state its present appearance. When French explorers and English fur traders first came to the area in the seventeenth century, they found numerous groups of Native Americans already farming the land.

The United States acquired the land from France as part of the Louisiana Purchase in 1803. It was the Lewis and Clark Expedition in 1804 that brought outsiders through the area for the first time. Yet Native Americans controlled the region throughout the first third of the nineteenth century. There was trading between the two cultures, but virtually no settlement. By 1830, however, large numbers of settlers were living east of the Mississippi River. Soon, battles erupted between Native Americans and the settlers. Federal troops were called in, and during the next twenty years, the Native American groups were forced to give up most of the land on the Iowa side of the river. By 1851, the last of the Native American groups, the Dakota, moved west into Kansas, Nebraska, and the Dakotas.

By that time, Iowa had become the twenty-ninth state, having joined the Union on December 28, 1846. Farming was already becoming the dominant way of life. Potatoes, wheat, and corn were the three most important crops in the first decades of state-hood. During the Civil War (1861–65), Iowa was on the side of the Union. The state supplied more soldiers per capita to the Union Army than any other state, with about 80,000 Iowans taking up arms.

After the war, farm prices dropped. Farms in the southern United States had resumed regular production, and farmers moving farther west began cultivating crops on the Great Plains. This led to a difficult period for Iowa's farmers, with many going heavily into debt. Farmers tried to unite, and supported politicians who would champion their cause. Although farming was still the way of life in Iowa, the protests lasted until about 1900, when prices for farm products began to increase.

In 1900, 75 percent of Iowans lived in rural areas. It was the invention of the automobile that began reducing the isolation of Iowa's farm families. Automobiles also brought about the need for good roads. During the spring thaw and in times of heavy rains, dirt roads were often impassable for days at a time. Life was changing. Still, it took

the creation of the Rural Electrification Administration in 1936 to finally bring electrical power to many rural parts of the state.

Both world wars led to rising farm prices and helped boost the economy, especially after the Great Depression of the 1930s. Yet in the 1950s and 1960s, the population of Iowa grew more slowly than in most other areas of the country. In fact, Iowa lost a seat in the House of Representatives in 1960, another in 1970, and a third in 1990.

Much of Iowa's economy has always been tied to farming. When prices for farm products fell between 1978 and 1987, more than 16,000 farms went out of business. The value of the land began rising again in 1987, only to be sidetracked by a disastrous drought in 1988 and record floods in 1993. In response, the state has developed some healthy non-farm industries. Des Moines, the capital and largest city, is one of the two leading centers for the insurance industry in the United States. In 1991, legal riverboat gambling began in Iowa as another way to create a larger tourist industry.

Not surprisingly, in a state with so much

MADISON COUNTY BRIDGES

There are six covered bridges listed as national historic places in Madison County. They were the setting for the popular motion picture *The Bridges of Madison County*.

open space, hunting and fishing are the most popular forms of outdoor recreation. There are many state-owned hunting areas open to the public. In addition, camping, hiking, riding, and water sports attract large numbers of people to the many state parks.

Hay gathering

A TRADITION IN THEATER AND MUSIC

Despite its reputation as a farm state, Iowa also has a great tradition in both the theater and music. In 1915, Iowa-born playwright Susan Glaspell and her husband, George Cram Cook, were instrumental in establishing the famous Provincetown Players, a group that became one of the most important in New York City in the 1920s. In 1931, Glaspell won a Pulitzer Prize for her play *Alison's House.*

The popular musical *The Music Man,* by Meredith Willson, was set in a small town in Iowa at the beginning of the twentieth century. Other Iowans who achieved musical fame include jazz trumpeter Bix Beiderbecke and bandleader Glenn Miller.

BUILDING A NEW STATE

From the time it was admitted as the twenty-ninth state on December 28, 1846, until the eve of the Civil War in 1861, Iowa saw the kind of growth that would shape the history of the state for the next 100 years. Once word of the fertile farmlands became widespread, immigrants fleeing revolutions and famines in Europe came to American and began looking for cheap farmland. Germans were the largest ethnic group in Iowa, followed by the Irish. The birth rate also exploded. By 1860, the population was triple what it had been ten years earlier. At that time, nearly one Iowan in two was under the age of ten. Sawmills were built along the Mississippi so that logs from Wisconsin and Minnesota could be turned into lumber for the farmers settling on the treeless prairies. All contributed to the growth of the new state.

Other Things to Know About Iowa

- The railroad bridge built in 1856 between Davenport and Rock Island was the first bridge to span the Mississippi River.
- Buffalo Bill Cody, the famous frontiersman and later organizer of Wild West shows, was born in Iowa in 1846.
- The largest popcorn-packing plant in the United States is located in Iowa.
- Herbert Hoover, the thirty-first president of the United States, was born in West Branch, Iowa, on August 10, 1874. His birthplace and boyhood neighborhood are preserved within the Herbert Hoover National Historic Site.
- The famous abolitionist John Brown used Iowa as a base for some of his antislavery activities prior to the Civil War.
- When Iowa provided some 80,000 soldiers to the Union cause during the Civil War, many women kept the family farms running while their husbands and sons were in battle.

NATURAL RESOURCES: corn, soybeans, hay, hogs, beef cattle, clay, gypsum, limestone, sand and gravel, and shale

MANUFACTURED PRODUCTS: industrial machinery, food products, electric and electronic equipment, metal, rubber, and plastic products, and printing materials

WILDLIFE: white-tailed deer, coyote, beaver, badger, weasel, mink, gray fox, three kinds of poisonous snakes, bald eagle, and a variety of fish

KANSAS

State bird: Eastern goldfinch

Before Alaska and Hawaii became states in 1959, the official geographical center of the United States was located near Lebanon, Kansas. In fact, Kansas is smack-dab in the middle of the country. Named for the Kansa people, who once lived in the northeastern part of the state, the name Kansas means "people of the south wind." For many years now, the state has led all others in the production of wheat and is often called the Breadbasket of the Nation.

While Kansas is part of America's Great Plains, it isn't entirely flat. The surface elevation increases gradually from east to west. There are hills, ridges, and wooded river valleys in eastern and central Kansas. In the western section, however, the land is a flatter, generally treeless high plain. Because of this flatness and the lack of trees, in periods of severe drought, the combination of hot days and high winds can create great dust storms, reminiscent of the Dust Bowl days of the 1930s.

Following the Louisiana Purchase in 1803, which gave the area to the United States, the Lewis and Clark Expedition began to explore the territory in 1804. Then, in 1806, Zebulon Pike led an expedition that crossed Kansas from east to west. He reported that the Great Plains were largely uninhabitable and that settlement should be confined east of the Mississippi River. Due to this feeling that the territory was unfit for white settlement, Congress passed legislation in 1830 and 1834 that allocated large portions of eastern Kansas to be used for the resettlement of Native Americans from the east. This relocation continued into the 1840s.

By the 1850s, however, the demand for land had increased, and Congress began to reconsider white settlement in the Kansas and Nebraska territories. The Kansas-Nebraska Act, passed in 1854, created separate Kansas and Nebraska territories and allowed the inhabitants to decide for themselves whether to allow slavery in the territory. This began a tumultuous period in which Native Americans were moved out and pro- and antislavery factions battled each other.

In January of 1861, Kansas became the thirty-fourth state of the Union, with Topeka as the state capital. Within months, however, the nation was engaged in the

Civil War (1861–65). Two-thirds of adult white males in the state (more than 20,000 men) fought on the side of the Union. Blacks and Native Americans from Kansas also served. Though there were no major battles fought in Kansas, the state suffered many bloody raids by Confederate soldiers.

The decades after the war saw the most intensive period of settlement in the state's history. Between 1860 and 1890, the population increased from about 100,000 to 1.4 million. In fact, the growth between 1870 and 1890 was greater than the population growth for the next eighty years. With the huge arrival of settlers, the central and western parts of the state became populated for the first time. Many of these people found life on the plains difficult. There were raids by Native Americans, droughts, blizzards, and plagues of grasshoppers (called locusts). Many people abandoned their new farms and moved elsewhere.

Gradually, however, the settlers adapted. Drought-resistant crops were developed, as

FRONT STREET

Old Front Street and the Boot Hill Museum in Dodge City are replicas of the way these places looked during the Wild West days of the late 1870s.

well as new agricultural techniques. Sod was used for building houses in the absence of lumber, while buffalo and cow manure were used for fuel. Windmills had the ability to bring water up from deep wells, and irrigation in the western part of the state became a way of life.

By the turn of the century, the state was prospering. Between 1900 and 1930, agricultural production continued to grow rapidly. Kansas became one of the leading wheat-producing regions in America. Things turned bad, however, during the Great Depression of the 1930s, as a major drought led to soil erosion on the plains. Winds brought swirling dust storms. The area became known as the Dust Bowl, and thousands were forced to abandon their farms. When rainfall increased later in the decade, the region began to recover with the help of government conservation programs.

The demand for farm products during the years of World War II (1939–45) increased, and the state began to expand industrial production to aid the war effort. This allowed the Kansas economy to become less dependent on agriculture. Though more small farms disappeared in the later decades of the twentieth century, larger and more mechanized farms increased production. By 1970, nearly two-thirds of Kansans lived in cities and towns. The rural population began to increase again, however, in the 1990s. With more manufacturing and high-tech companies, people moved to the rural communities and commuted to work—a situation typical throughout America.

Today, in eastern Kansas, there is continued construction of new manufacturing plants, as well as large corporate headquarters for insurance and communication companies. Diversity has kept unemployment rates low. Kansas has become very much a modern state while it continues to be the Breadbasket of the Nation.

Buffalo and elk, which once roamed freely on the Kansas plains, are now preserved in wildlife management areas and on private ranches.

Other Things to Know About Kansas

- The carousel with jumping horses was invented in Kansas in 1898.
- During the nineteenth century, two of the most famous overland routes in U.S. history, the Santa Fe Trail and the Oregon Trail, extended across parts of what is now Kansas.
- In the 1820s and 1830s, missionaries established the first schools in Kansas to instruct Native Americans in reading and writing, and to try to convert them to Christianity.
- The Native Americans who lived in Kansas in the eighteenth and nineteenth centuries were on the move constantly in pursuit of buffalo herds. They traveled almost exclusively on horseback and were among the best riders in North America.
- In 1990, Democrat Joan Finney was the first woman to be elected governor of Kansas

NATURAL RESOURCES: wheat, sorghum, soybeans, corn, beef cattle, hogs, natural gas, helium, hydrogen, petroleum, salt, sand and gravel, and stone

MANUFACTURED PRODUCTS: aircraft and other transportation equipment, industrial machinery, chemicals, electric and electronic equipment, processed food, petroleum, printed materials, and metal, coal, rubber, and plastic products

WILDLIFE: deer, coyote, red fox, badger, black-tailed prairie dog, raccoon, copperhead snake, rattlesnake, a variety of small birds and non-poisonous snakes

KENTUCKY

State bird: Cardinal

The name Kentucky comes from a Native American term for the area south of the Ohio River. It is believed to mean "meadowland," and was spelled and pronounced several ways over the years. Early pioneers referred to Kaintuckee and Cantuckey when they spoke of the region. But as soon as people hear the familiar strains of the song, "My Old Kentucky Home," there is no mistaking the nation's fifteenth state and its revered traditions.

Located in the east central United States with Illinois, Indiana, and Ohio to the north and Tennessee to the south, Kentucky has absorbed elements of both the north and the south. As the first state west of the Appalachian Mountains, Kentucky also has links to the original thirteen colonies. The grass grown in the pastures of central Kentucky has buds with a purplish-blue hue, which accounts for its nickname, The Bluegrass State.

Before Kentucky was settled, the entire region was almost completely covered by forest. The first explorers came through the region in the 1670s and 1680s, but after that, there were no efforts to explore the region for many years. When the French and Indian War (1754–63) ended, a treaty gave Great Britain all the territory east of the Mississippi, including what is now Kentucky. That was when a number of frontiersmen began coming into the territory. They were called "long hunters" because of their extended hunting trips.

The most famous of these men was the legendary Daniel Boone, from Pennsylvania. Boone first came to Kentucky in 1767 and 1768 to hunt and trap. He also wanted to find a route to the bluegrass region of central and northern Kentucky. He explored and hunted in much of the territory until 1771. James Harrod, however, founded the first permanent settlement in Kentucky in 1774. A year later, Daniel Boone returned to found Boonesborough on the Kentucky River, about forty-five miles east of Harrodstown.

There were some early battles between settlers and the Native Americans who already lived in the area. Then, during the American Revolution (1775–83), there were a couple of skirmishes with both the British and their Native American allies. Shortly after America won its freedom, thousands of settlers began migrating from the East down the Ohio River and into Kentucky. By 1790, the region had a population of more than 73,000, and two years later, it became the fifteenth state. By 1818, the final Native

American claims to Kentucky lands were eliminated, and in the first half of the nineteenth century, the state developed a large agricultural economy, growing hemp and tobacco. Manufacturing also grew, as did the population. By 1860, there were 1,155,684 people living in the state.

Throughout the Civil War (1861–65), Kentucky was divided. There were some 225,000 slaves in Kentucky, yet many of the whites living there opposed slavery and had little sympathy with the South. The state tried to stay neutral, with the legislature resolving that Kentucky would take no part in the fighting. Because of its location, however, both the Union and the Confederate sides wanted a foothold in Kentucky. The state was at the mercy of occupying armies throughout the war, with several major battles fought there.

Mammoth Cave in Mammoth Cave National Park is the longest explored cave system in the world.

Eventually, Kentuckians fought on both sides of the conflict, even after the legislature aligned the state with the Union in 1862. Yet blacks didn't become legally free until the Thirteenth Amendment to the Constitution became law in December 1865, eight months after the war's end. Kentucky was the perfect example of a state whose location caused conflicting feelings among its residents.

Labor-management problems in the mining industry plagued the state in the early decades of the twentieth century, with violence erupting on several occasions. Tobacco farming flourished, and the timber industry grew. But coal mining created bitterness between labor and management that lasted for years. In the 1950s, Kentucky—like other southern states—still had segregation in education. However, when the Supreme Court ruling of 1954 declared segregation illegal, the state integrated quickly and with minimal problems.

There were still other problems to be

addressed. In 1960, the state's per-capita income was only 71 percent of the national average. And in 1970, Kentucky was the last of all the states in the number of school years adult residents had completed—an average of 9.9 years as opposed to the national average of 12.1. Part of the reason was the poor economy, as the state began changing from an agricultural and mining base to manufacturing. More recently, Kentucky's economy has depended more upon electronics, machinery, textiles, and the metal and chemical industries.

THE KENTUCKY DERBY

Thoroughbred horses have been bred and raised in Kentucky for generations. There are races held in the state continuously from spring to fall. But none have the tradition of the Kentucky Derby—the most famous horse race in America. The annual Derby has been held at Louisville's Churchill Downs on the first Saturday in May since 1875. People flock to Louisville for the two-week Kentucky Derby Festival, making the race and its surroundings a source of gala entertainment for thousands upon thousands of fans.

Today, Kentucky has struck a balance between the past and present, between old traditions and the technology of the twenty-first century. Louisville and Lexington are the two largest cities, with populations in the mid-200,000 range, while smaller Frankfort is the state capital. Those who visit the state can see a combination of the beauty and tradition of the past with all the innovations of the modern world.

Other Things to Know About Kentucky

- The world's largest braille publishing house is located in Kentucky.
- The Abraham Lincoln Birthplace National Historic Site, located near Hodgenville, includes the log cabin where the sixteenth president was born.
- At the My Old Kentucky Home State Park is the mansion called Federal Hill, where Pennsylvanian Stephen Foster was inspired to write the famous song for which the park is named.
- Kentucky was the only state represented in the cabinets of both the Union and Confederate governments during the Civil War. James Speed was the Union attorney general, while John Cabell Breckinridge was the Confederate secretary of war.
- The first African American elected to a Southern legislature after post–Civil War Reconstruction was in Kentucky, in the 1930s.
- At Cumberland Falls State Park is a sixty-eight-foot high waterfall that makes a "moonbow," a kind of rainbow at night.

NATURAL RESOURCES: tobacco, corn, soybeans, beef cattle, eggs, hay, hogs, milk, coal, natural gas, petroleum, sand and gravel, stone, thoroughbred horses

MANUFACTURED PRODUCTS: electric and electronic equipment, transportation equipment, chemicals, metals, clothing, and metal, paper, rubber, and plastic products

WILDLIFE: white-tailed deer, black bear (rare), red wolf (reintroduced), red fox, gray fox, mink, muskrat, a large variety of fish and birds, rattle snake, copperhead, and cottonmouth snakes, and turtles and lizards

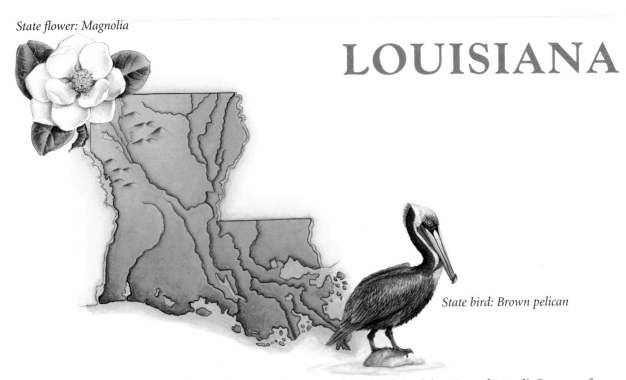

State flower: Magnolia

LOUISIANA

State bird: Brown pelican

The mention of Louisiana often conjures up images of the colorful celebration of Mardi Gras or of traditional jazz bands playing the kind of music that had its birth in the city of New Orleans at the beginning of the twentieth century. While those events are a definite part of Louisiana's history, the story of the state is much deeper and multilayered. Bordered by Texas to the west, Arkansas to the north, Mississippi to the east, and the Gulf of Mexico to the south, Louisiana is part of America's deep southern tradition. Yet the territory—once controlled by France, Great Britain, and Spain—has both European and African influences as part of its rich history.

From the earliest days of settlement until today, Louisiana has seen its share of hard times.

In 1682, the French explorer René-Robert Cavelier, Sieur de la Salle, traveled down the Mississippi River to its mouth and claimed all the land by the river and its tributaries for France. He named the vast region *Louisiane* in honor of the reigning French king, Louis XIV. Soon the French were building forts and settlements along the Gulf Coast and in the Mississippi Valley. One of the settlements, Nouvelle-Orléans, was established in 1718 to secure the lower Mississippi against colonial rivals Spain and Great Britain.

Louisiana remained a French colony until 1762, when France transferred it to Spain during the French and Indian War with Great Britain (1754–63). During Spanish rule over the next thirty-four years, immigrants from Spain as well as French-speaking refugees from France, Canada, and the West Indies settled in the area. People also came from the island of Saint-Domingue (present-day Haiti), and from eastern Canada. These people were called Acadians, and once in Louisiana, they became known as Cajuns. They soon became the dominant cultural group in rural southern Louisiana. In addition, more black slaves were brought over from Africa. A melting-pot culture was beginning to form.

The territory became part of the United States with the Louisiana Purchase in 1803. Nine years later, on April 30, 1812, the Territory of Orleans entered the Union as the state of Louisiana, the nation's eighteenth state. It was not until after the War of 1812 with Great Britain (1812–15) that settlers began to arrive in large numbers. By 1820, there were about 153,000 residents, with the numbers growing to 708,000 in 1860. About half of them were black slaves.

Louisiana was one of the states seceding from the Union at the start of the Civil War (1861–65). However, even before the war ended, a new state constitution was drafted that abolished slavery. But as in other states in the Deep South, old ways died hard. There were race riots and lynchings, and attempts by various white groups to deny blacks any rights. Because of this, the federal army occupied the state until 1877.

By the 1880s, the state was producing large crops of cotton, rice, and sugarcane. But farm prices were often low, and there was still much poverty, especially in rural areas. The opening of the Panama Canal in 1914 stimulated growth in the city of New Orleans, and it soon became one of the nation's leading ports. The state's economy was further stimulated by the discovery of large oil deposits and sources of natural gas. This resulted in an increase in industrial activity, helping to take away some of the state's dependence on agriculture.

Louisiana, like many of the southern states, looked for ways to ignore the 1954 Supreme Court decision that made public school segregation unconstitutional. The state legislature passed its own laws, which subsequently were declared unconstitutional. Integration took place slowly during the early 1960s. There were boycotts and some riots, leading to much negative publicity for the state. It wasn't until about 1971 that the legality of equal rights for African Americans was finally settled.

The 1970s saw unprecedented economic prosperity as the result of the oil boom. But when the industry ran into tough times in the 1980s, so did the state. There were also new political scandals and divided feelings over state-sanctioned gambling, a way some saw to bolster the economy. It wasn't until the 1990s that a combination of growth in the mining, agricultural, lumbering, and fishing industries provided the basis for increased manufacturing and a stabilizing economy.

MARDI GRAS

The name is French for "Fat Tuesday," and describes a pre-Lenten festival celebrated in Roman Catholic communities. Strictly speaking, Mardi Gras is celebrated by the French and is a time of preparation immediately before Ash Wednesday and the start of the fast of Lent. It is a last opportunity for merrymaking and indulgence in food and drink. Today, Mardi Gras is generally celebrated for a full week before Lent and is marked by spectacular parades featuring floats, pageants, elaborate costumes, masked balls, and dancing in the streets. New Orleans is the home of the most festive celebration in America. Thousands of people flock to the city each year in anticipation of a good time. Over the years, Mardi Gras has become synonymous with New Orleans.

New Orleans continues to be a wondrous place for tourists, especially at Mardi Gras time. The city also has many remnants of the past, of a time when the influences of several different cultures all blended together to make New Orleans one of the most interesting places in the country.

Other Things to Know About Louisiana

- The Lake Pontchartrain Causeway at New Orleans is the longest bridge in the United States; it is almost twenty-four miles long.
- Jean Lafitte National Historical Park near New Orleans marks the site of the Battle of New Orleans, where General Andrew Jackson's troops defeated the British in 1815 to end the War of 1812. Lafitte was an infamous pirate of the time who brought his men ashore to help Jackson's troops in the battle.
- There are still a substantial number of French inhabitants in Louisiana. Creoles are descended from the French, some Spanish, and a few German settlers from the eighteenth century. Cajuns were originally the Acadian people from Nova Scotia. The two groups have partially merged and retain much of their original culture, including the French language.
- The Audubon memorial in the south central part of the state is the site of the plantation home once occupied by famous wildlife painter John James Audubon.
- New Orleans is the state's largest city, with 485,000 inhabitants. The state capital, Baton Rouge, is the second largest city, with more than 200,000 residents.

NATURAL RESOURCES: cotton, rice, sugarcane, soybeans, beef cattle, pecans, sweet potatoes, petroleum, natural gas, salt, sulfur, catfish, crawfish, oysters, and shrimp

MANUFACTURED PRODUCTS: chemicals, processed food, lumber, machinery, printing and publishing, transportation equipment, and coal, metal, wood, petroleum, and paper products

WILDLIFE: white-tailed deer, black bear, mink, raccoon, wildcat, gray fox, weasel, alligators, turtles, lizards, snakes (poisonous and non-poisonous), and a large variety of game fish. More than half the species of birds in North America are either residents of the state, or spend a portion of their migration there.

The state tree of Louisiana is the bald cypress.

THE BIRTH OF JAZZ

In the opinion of many, jazz music is the only original art form to be born in America. New Orleans is generally acknowledged as the birthplace of jazz—a music based on the ability to use life experience in soulful improvisation. The early part of the twentieth century featured small groups playing a largely ensemble style. It was the trumpet playing of New Orleans–born Louis Armstrong that began to take the music more toward a soloist's art. Armstrong would go on to become famous throughout the world—and arguably the most influential figure in all of American music, instrumental and vocal. Other outstanding early jazz musicians born in New Orleans were cornetist Joe "King" Oliver and soprano saxophonist/clarinetist Sidney Bechet.

State flower: White pine cone and tassel

MAINE

State bird: Chickadee

Nestled in the northeastern corner of the United States, the state of Maine is the first place in America to see the sun rise every morning. A land of natural beauty, with forests, lakes, and rivers, Maine is often the place people think about when they want to "get away from it all." While much of the land still appears unspoiled in a state considered the third most rural in the country, Maine had an early history that was rife with turbulence and uncertainty.

Though Europeans first arrived in the sixteenth century, early settlement in Maine was not easy—and not without dispute. The French and the English were constantly competing for the territory; they had their first conflict at Mount Desert Island early in the seventeenth century. It set the stage for on-and-off warfare in Maine between the two countries that would last almost 150 years. Early settlement was also made difficult by disputes over land titles, with Native Americans making claims along with French and English settlers.

Though it was a harsh land, the early European settlers depended on fishing, farming, furs, and lumbering to earn a living. Fishermen would make their catch along the Maine coast, then sun-dry or salt the fish before taking it back to Europe. By 1650, the few permanent settlements in Maine were located along the coast. They moved inland only if there was a river for transportation.

Throughout the seventeenth and into the eighteenth centuries, wars between Great Britain and France led to hostilities in Maine. Finally, at the end of the French and Indian War (1754–63), resistance by both the French and Native Americans to English settlement stopped. Between 1765 and 1775, the population of the area doubled, from 23,000 to 47,000 settlers.

After the American Revolution (1775–83), there was a movement to separate Maine from Massachusetts. When that was done (during the War of 1812), there was great interest in making Maine a state. Finally, in 1820, Maine became the twenty-third state as part of the Missouri Compromise. This allowed Maine to enter the Union as a free state to balance the entrance of Missouri as a slave state.

Maine continued to grow, and was staunchly on the side of the Union during the Civil War (1861–65). There were many troops in the fighting and a number of heroes from the state. For the remainder of the century after the war, Maine's economy relied on its natural resources—fish, granite, ice, and wood. Much of the work, however, was seasonal, so many of the state's residents lived with very low salaries and tough working conditions.

The shipbuilding industry flourished in Maine throughout the nineteenth century. With the abundance of wood, workers built clipper ships, schooners, and large commercial ships that transported the state's products. When ships began to be made from iron and steel, the call for wooden ships declined. But the Bath Iron Works in southern Maine soon opened, and its workers began making modern ships, including 236 Liberty ships during World War II (1939–45). In the years following the war, most states experienced economic and population growth. Maine, however, went the other way. The economy faltered and the

Moose

population declined, as more people left the state to look for jobs elsewhere. Economic woes led to problems in education, health, and other social services.

The situation began to improve after the election of Edmund Muskie as governor in 1954, then U.S. senator in 1958. Muskie worked to create more job opportunities and to improving the educational system. He also began a movement that led to environmental legislation in the 1960s and 1970s to protect the natural beauty of the state. This led to the development of tourism as a major industry. But more people can lead to more pollution. The state has had to maintain a delicate balance between keeping nature unspoiled and bolstering its economy.

TAKING THE ROADS

The state of Maine has virtually no passenger service on its few railroads. Most service was gradually terminated over the years, as were railroad operations in general. There are some 22,510 miles of highways in the state, as compared to just 1,121 miles of rails, owned by small regional and local companies. All residents and tourists have to travel by car or bus, while trucks haul most of the freight. The networks of roads are dense in the heavily settled southwestern part of the state, but very sparse in the north. In fact, the northwestern sector of Maine is served almost exclusively by private roads, which are owned and maintained by large forest owners. People traveling these roads must pay a fee. Because residents must travel by car, there are a number of auto ferries operating in the state, taking cars between Bar Harbor and Yarmouth, Nova Scotia; between Portland and Yarmouth; and to many of the offshore islands.

West Quoddy Head, Maine, is the easternmost point in the United States.

Stonington is a village on the southernmost tip of Deer Isle.

Native Americans also filed suit to recover lands in Maine they said were taken illegally. In a 1980 settlement, the U.S. government paid Maine's Native Americans $81.5 million to give up their claims to the land. The group then used the money to purchase 300,000 acres and invest in a variety of businesses. This, too, helped the overall economy of a state that has always had to struggle.

Many people moved to Maine in the latter years of the twentieth century, looking for a more simple lifestyle. Though Maine still retains its beauty and is an attractive haven for newcomers, some natives of the state find it difficult to make a good living. Many residents are underemployed or depend on low-paying service jobs. The

challenge for the state, then, remains the same: to preserve the beauty of the land while bringing more and better-paying jobs to its people.

Other Things to Know About Maine

- The *Virginia*—the first successful ocean-going ship made in America—was built in Maine by settlers who tried to establish a colony in 1607. The colony was soon abandoned, but the *Virginia* sailed the seas for twenty years.
- Mount Katahdin, the highest spot in Maine (5,267 feet), is the first place in the United States that the sun hits in the morning.
- Though much of Maine's rocky soil and hilly terrain is unsuitable for agriculture, the state still ranks seventh in potato production in the nation.
- Maine's original white pine forest—which covered much of the state—was almost entirely cut away by the shipbuilding industry, beginning in colonial times. Today, tree farming has replaced the careless exploitation of forest resources.
- Maine has no large cities. Portland is the largest, with a population of just over 64,000 residents in 1998. Lewiston is next, with fewer than 40,000 people, followed by Bangor with about 33,000. It is safe to say that the entire state has something of a small-town atmosphere.
- The first library in Maine was founded at Kittery in 1751 by Sir William Pepperell.
- Burnham Tavern, in Machias, was used in 1775 as a meeting place by local patriots planning the first naval battle of the American Revolution. Today, it is a museum and tourist attraction.

NATURAL RESOURCES: wood, potatoes, milk, eggs, fish, seafood, apples, beef cattle, blueberries, clams, cod, lobster, haddock, sardines, gemstones, sand and gravel, and stone

MANUFACTURED PRODUCTS: transportation equipment, electronic equipment, footwear, clothing, leather products, processed food, machinery, pulp and paper, ships and boats, and textiles

WILDLIFE: white-tailed deer, black bear, moose, beaver, lynx, bobcat, coyote, fox, mink, weasel; a large variety of birds, including ruffed grouse, woodcock, and wild turkey; a large variety of both fresh and saltwater fish, lobsters, clams, scallops, and shrimp

---

CIVIL WAR HEROES

Though there was very little fighting in Maine during the Civil War, the state nevertheless contributed mightily to the Union victory. Some 73,000 Maine residents fought in the conflict, with its regiments playing key roles in a number of battles, notably the Battle of Gettysburg. Maine natives General Joshua Chamberlain and General Oliver Otis Howard distinguished themselves during the war, while fellow native Hannibal Hamlin served as vice president under Abraham Lincoln from 1861 to 1865. William Fessenden, a U.S. senator from Maine, became Lincoln's secretary of the treasury in 1864.

MARYLAND

State bird: Baltimore oriole

One of America's original thirteen states, Maryland was founded as a colony in 1634 and was named after Queen Henrietta Maria, the wife of King Charles I of England. Ranking forty-second in size, the state is situated just below Pennsylvania. Delaware and the Atlantic Ocean border it on the east, while Virginia sits to the south and West Virginia to the southwest and west. The nation's capital, Washington, D.C., is located in an enclave along the Maryland-Virginia border. This fact alone gives Maryland a prominent place in the country's history.

The Chesapeake Bay—a large inlet of the Atlantic Ocean—divides the state into two distinct sections. The section east of the bay, which is known as the Eastern Shore, is part of the Delmarva Peninsula. The Western Shore, on the other side of the bay, is the site of both the state capital, Annapolis, and the state's largest city, Baltimore. Washington, D.C., is also just off the Western Shore, on the western side of the Potomac River.

William Claiborne built the first white settlement in Maryland in 1631. It was a fur trading post on Kent Island, just east of present-day Annapolis. The settlement was paid for by a commercial license issued by neighboring Virginia. A year later, King Charles granted George Calvert the land north of the Potomac River, which had been originally granted to the Virginia Colony. Calvert wanted to establish a community where those of the Catholic faith, who were persecuted in England, could worship freely.

Settlers planted corn and tobacco, traded with Native Americans, and seemed to be thriving.

By 1638, however, fighting broke out between the Claiborne and Calvert factions. These conflicts would continue on and off for many years, much of it between rival religious groups. Despite the threat of violence that lasted for decades, people continued to come to the area. By century's end, settlers had spread over much of Maryland, especially along the rivers and creeks that allowed access to the ocean. Tobacco was a major crop, and many of the farmers began using black slaves to work their farms.

When the Declaration of Independence was drafted late in the eighteenth century, Maryland delegates voted in favor of it. After the war for independence, Maryland became the seventh state to ratify the Constitution, doing so on April 28, 1788. By this time, wheat had surpassed tobacco as the state's primary crop, creating the wealth that allowed the city of Baltimore to grow rapidly. There were mills built to refine flour, warehouses along the docks, and ships constructed to aid with exports. Wheat had spawned an entire industry.

Maryland was a target during the War of 1812 (1812–15) because of its proximity to the nation's capital. British ships sailed into Chesapeake Bay and began attacking communities along the shore. Soon British troops entered Washington and burned a number of buildings, including the White House. The British subsequently threatened Baltimore, but were stopped before they could enter the city.

After the war, Baltimore continued to grow. By the 1850s, the Baltimore and Ohio Railroad was helping to bring continuing prosperity to much of the state. By 1860, the city had a population of about 212,000—nearly a third of the population of the state. A year later, the Civil War (1861–65) broke out. The state's 14,000 slaveholders wanted to secede and have Maryland become part of the Confederacy. But because Maryland was so near to Washington, President Lincoln wanted to be sure it remained in the Union. Troops were sent quickly, and Baltimore was occupied for nearly the entire war. Some 50,000 Marylanders fought on the Union side, while about 22,000 volunteered on the Confederate side.

Maryland was the first state to abolish slavery on its own, in 1864. There were also three major Civil War battles in the state, including the bloody Battle of Antietam. After the war and for the remainder of the nineteenth century, the state's economy grew unevenly. Baltimore lost its top spot in flour milling to the new Western Wheat Belt, and the economy of the city shifted to clothing, canning, fertilizer, steel, and coastal shipping.

When the United States entered World War I (1914–18) in 1917, the War Department and the navy took large tracts of land in the state for training camps and weapons testing grounds. Military production boosted the economy once again. The same thing occurred during World War II (1939–45), as industries such as shipbuilding worked around the clock. After the war, the economy continued to grow and prosper.

In the 1960s, the Civil Rights movement led to unrest in several Maryland cities, but the old ways soon began to disappear. The economy began shifting in the 1960s and 1970s from heavy to light industry, with more high-tech firms becoming established in the state. By the 1990s, however, Maryland was again somewhat divided economically. Baltimore, like many large cities, had financial problems and too many people working for low wages. Many of the wealthier people lived in various suburban areas. So the state once again has to improve its economy in the twenty-first century and, like many others, work on closing the gap between the rich and poor.

THE STAR-SPANGLED BANNER

During the War of 1812, British troops and ships focused on Maryland as a strategic area to control. In August 1814, the British burned the White House in Washington. Then, on September 13, British warships attacked Fort McHenry, which guarded the entrance to Baltimore Harbor. For twenty-five straight hours, British cannon bombarded the fort, but the American defenders would not surrender. The next day, British ships finally withdrew. An observer of the siege was Maryland lawyer and poet, Francis Scott Key, who watched from a boat in the harbor. When the smoke cleared and Key saw the American flag still flying, he was inspired to write a poem. "The Star-Spangled Banner" was set to music and, in 1931, officially become the nation's national anthem.

SHELLFISH OF THE CHESAPEAKE

Maryland is known for its shellfish, especially those harvested from the Chesapeake Bay. Since the mid-1960s, it has been one of the top-ranked states in the number of oysters taken annually. Other important Maryland shellfish include clams and blue crabs. Clams have traditionally been sent to many New England restaurants, where they are served as delicacies, either fried or steamed. There is evidence, however, that harvesting of both shellfish and fish may have to be restricted. The total catch of Maryland's fisheries (which accounts for everything taken from the Bay) in the early 1990s was about one-half the level of the early 1980s.

- Maryland is the narrowest state in the Union. At one point, near the town of Hancock, the state is only one mile wide.
- The first publicly supported school in the colony of Maryland was King William's School, established at Annapolis in 1696.
- The Babe Ruth Birthplace and Baseball Center is located in Baltimore, the birthplace of the Hall of Fame Yankees slugger. It has exhibits and films about the man whom many still consider to have been the greatest baseball player ever.
- The Preakness Stakes, the second part of horse racing's famed Triple Crown, is run at Baltimore's Pimlico Race Track each May, after the Kentucky Derby and before the Belmont Stakes.

NATURAL RESOURCES: chicken, corn, beef cattle, fruit, milk, soybeans, blue crabs, softshell crabs, oysters, clams, clay, coal, sand and gravel, and stone

MANUFACTURED PRODUCTS: chemicals, electric and electronic equipment, processed food, machinery, printing and publishing, and transportation equipment

WILDLIFE: white-tailed deer, black bear, red fox, raccoon, otter, muskrat, mink, fish, shellfish, waterfowl, and a variety of snakes and birds

Annapolis is the home of the U.S. Naval Academy. It was founded originally in 1845 as a naval school and was reorganized and renamed in 1851.

MASSACHUSETTS

State bird: Chickadee

One of the first areas of America to be settled by Europeans, Massachusetts has a long and colorful history. The sixth state to be admitted to the Union as part of the original thirteen, this New England state played a major role in the country's fight for independence from Great Britain. In fact, Massachusetts has played a major role in almost every conflict and turning point in the entire history of the United States.

The Bay State is filled with historic landmarks and famous intellectual institutions. It was the birthplace of four presidents, and houses one of the major cities in the United States—Boston. It is also known for its summer resorts, such as the peninsula of Cape Cod, and the islands of Nantucket and Martha's Vineyard. At the restored Plymouth Plantation, visitors can see what life was like in colonial America, as well as view a replica of the *Mayflower,* the vessel that brought the first Pilgrims to Massachusetts in 1620.

Though the coast of Massachusetts had been explored a number of times early in the seventeenth century, the landing of the Pilgrims was the first attempt at colonization. The Pilgrims were a group of religious dissenters who had faced persecution in England and were looking for a new life in a new land. Their voyage wasn't easy. They had hoped to land in Virginia, but were blown off course and wound up in Massachusetts. Not prepared for the severe winter weather, more than half of them died the first year.

It wasn't until the Native Americans showed the Pilgrims how to grow corn and catch fish that life began getting easier. By 1628, a major colonization effort began, and the colony started growing steadily over the next half century. A war with Native Americans in 1675 halted Native American resistance to white settlement in southern New England. Over the next century, the colonists became involved in a number of wars between Great Britain and France, and they began to oppose the restrictions of British rule. Resistance by the colonies was spearheaded in Massachusetts by defiant acts such as the Boston Tea Party in 1773, when colonists dumped British tea into the harbor to protest high taxes.

The first battles of the American Revolution (1775–83) took place outside Boston in 1775, after Paul Revere made his famous ride to warn local patriots that "The British are coming!" The battles of Lexington and Concord followed, and the Revolution was under way. The British eventually

Statue of Paul Revere

A HISTORIC SPORTS TRADITION

Along with its other historical traditions, the state of Massachusetts has a rich history in American sports. Basketball—which may soon become the most popular sport in the entire world—was invented by Dr. James Naismith in Springfield in 1891. Four years later, volleyball was invented in Holyoke by William Morgan. American football was helped in its development in the early part of the twentieth century due largely to the vigorous way it was played at Massachusetts universities. There were still other firsts. The first professional golf tournament was held at Hamilton in 1901; the first World Series baseball game was played in Boston in 1903; and the first National Basketball Association All-Star game was held in Boston in 1951.

occupied Boston, until an army led by General George Washington forced them to evacuate in March 1776. After the war, the Constitution of the United States was drafted, and Massachusetts became the sixth state to ratify it on February 6, 1788.

Massachusetts had a thriving economy as the young nation's leading overseas trader. Whaling and shipping were prosperous industries. During and after the War of 1812 (1812–15), Massachusetts was one of the first states to establish new industries, becoming more of a manufacturing state. Textiles were one of the first mass-produced products.

Prior to the Civil War (1861–65), the state became known for its intense antislavery activities. The Underground Railroad—a network of secret locations—brought many runaway slaves through Massachusetts on their way to Canada. The state was the first to send troops to support the federal government during the war, and later, the Fifty-fourth Massachusetts Regiment became the first African American regiment to serve the Union cause in battle. After the war and into the early years of the twentieth century, there were occasional labor strikes and violence in the state, which had become one of the most industrialized in the nation.

Cranberry bog

When the United States entered World War I (1914–18) in 1917, shipyards in Boston and Quincy worked around the clock, and the state produced a wide variety of wartime supplies. As was the case in many states, the war produced an economic boom that lasted throughout the 1920s. The 1930s saw the Great Depression affect Massachusetts as well as the entire country, before World War II (1939–45) led to another robust recovery.

The election of John F. Kennedy as the nation's thirty-fifth president in 1960 once again focused attention on Massachusetts. The saga of the Kennedy family—including the assassinations of the president in 1963 and that of his brother Robert in 1968—would engross the nation for many years. The 1970s exposed racial problems in Boston, showing that cities in the East could have conflicts similar to those in the South.

At the outset of the twenty-first century, the state continues to evolve. Officials are trying to attract new businesses, correct gaps between rich and poor, and make the change from heavy industry to technology. Yet despite many changes, the long and colorful history of the state remains for all to see.

You can visit the USS *Constitution* in Boston.

Other Things to Know About Massachusetts

- The first college in any of the colonies was Harvard, which was founded in Cambridge in 1636.
- The first printing press in the colonies was brought to Cambridge by Stephen Daye in 1638.
- In the fall of 1621, a harvest of corn and beans, along with fish and game, was shared by the settlers and Native Americans in the first American Thanksgiving celebration.
- In the nineteenth century, Massachusetts became the center of a renaissance in literature, with writers such as Ralph Waldo Emerson, Henry David Thoreau, Nathaniel Hawthorne, and Henry Wadsworth Longfellow all gaining international and lasting fame.
- In 1987, the Gay Head Band of Wampanoag became the first Native American group in Massachusetts to gain federal recognition as a tribe.

NATURAL RESOURCES: eggs, milk, turkeys, fruits and vegetables, flowers and shrubs, cranberries, bluefish, cod, mackerel, lobster, scallops, sea bass, squid, swordfish, lime, sand and gravel, and stone

MANUFACTURED PRODUCTS: chemicals, clothing, computer hardware and software, electric and electronic equipment, instruments, machinery, metal products, plastics, printed materials, and textiles

WILDLIFE: white-tailed deer, black bear, fox, beaver, raccoon, more than 400 species of birds, and a large variety of freshwater and saltwater fish

---

THE KENNEDYS

Joseph P. Kennedy, a successful and wealthy businessman, saw a bright future for his four sons. His ambition knew no limits. He wanted his eldest son, Joseph P. Kennedy, Jr., to be president of the United States. However, Joe, Jr., was killed during an air mission in World War II. But in 1960, the second eldest son, John F. Kennedy, already a Democratic senator from Massachusetts, was elected President of the United States. This began a political era that was called an American Camelot. It was also rife with tragedy. President Kennedy was assassinated in 1963. His younger brother Robert F. Kennedy (himself a former U.S. attorney general and senator from New York) was assassinated in 1968 while seeking the Democratic nomination for president. The youngest son, Edward M. Kennedy, has been a longtime Massachusetts senator, while members of the next generation of Kennedys have also entered public service, continuing the family tradition.

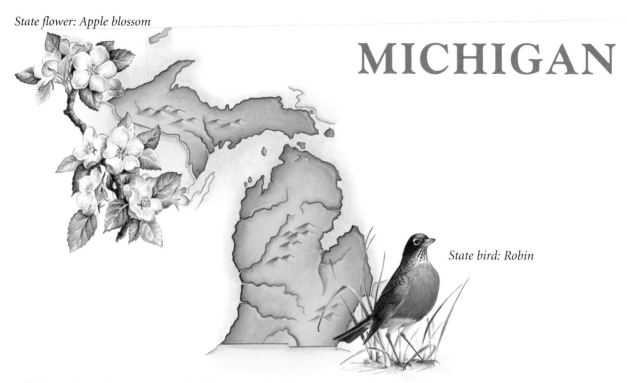

State flower: Apple blossom

MICHIGAN

State bird: Robin

Michigan is unique among the fifty states because it is the only one consisting of two peninsulas that are completely separated by water. The southern part of the Lower Peninsula borders on Ohio and Indiana, while the western portion of the Upper Peninsula sits alongside Wisconsin. All other sections of both peninsulas border on water, touching on four of the five Great Lakes, while the Straits of Mackinac separate the two peninsulas. The name Michigan *comes from the Chippewa word* micigama, *which means "great water," and refers to Lake Michigan.*

In many ways, Michigan has made an amazing transformation in a relatively short amount of time. During much of the second half of the nineteenth century, the state was still heavily forested. The need for lumber on the neighboring Plains states brought about an almost frenzied period of deforestation. By the start of the twentieth century, an extensive reforestation program was started, and the new and growing automobile industry soon moved the state into heavy industrialization.

The first permanent settlement in Michigan was established in 1668, when Father Jacques Marquette, a French priest and explorer, founded a mission at Sault Sainte Marie. Three years later, the French proclaimed the entire interior section of North America as part of New France. When the British took over the area at the end of the French and Indian War (1754–63), very few whites lived there. There was fur-trading activity there, but little else. When the American Revolution (1775–83) began, colonization in the Michigan woods was still minimal.

After the war, the land was part of several large divisions (the Northwest Territory and the Territory of Indiana) before the Michigan Territory was created on January 11, 1805. Detroit was its capital. Finally, on January 26, 1837, Michigan became the nation's twenty-sixth state. It began to grow rapidly, and by 1840 there were more than 212,000 people living there.

Lumber and mining were the first two successful industries. The opening of the Sault Sainte Marie Canals in 1855 made it possible for ships to pass between Lake Superior and the lower lakes, making it easier to ship products. Soon, however, the state of Michigan would have all normal life interrupted by the Civil War (1861–65).

Michigan was on the side of the Union, supplying troops for battle and also providing many stops on the Underground Railroad—the name given to the network of safe havens for fugitive slaves who were seeking safety in Canada. After the war, the state began making the transition from an agricultural to an industrial economy. Manufacturing had tripled in the fifteen years after the war ended, and by the turn of the century, manufacturing in Detroit alone exceeded the output of the entire state some thirty years earlier.

It was at about this time that the state of Michigan began to form the identity by which it would be known for much of the twentieth century. Automobile manufacturing began in the 1890s, with many of the men who had made fortunes in lumber and mining now investing in the automobile. Ransom E. Olds of Lansing established the first Michigan company to manufacture automobiles in 1897. The Ford Motor Company was founded by Henry Ford in 1903, with the first Model T produced in 1908.

With the automobile industry becoming firmly entrenched, the cities grew rapidly. By 1920, Detroit had a population of one million residents and had become the fourth largest city in the country. During World War I (1914–18), factories worked around the clock. Thousands of African Americans came to the city from the South looking for jobs and a better life. During World War II (1939–45), there was so much military equipment produced in Detroit that the city became known as the Arsenal of Democracy.

But there were difficulties after World War II. The automobile industry began to decline in the 1950s, and the 1960s saw both racial and economic problems, especially in the cities. There was a major racial riot in Detroit in 1967, during which blocks of buildings were burned and forty-three people were killed. The 1970s and 1980s saw the state trying to weather still more crises. Automobile plants were moving to the suburbs or out of state. There were high unemployment and deteriorating neighborhoods in the cities.

Finally, in the 1990s, the state began to

RECREATION EVERYWHERE

With 11,000 lakes, as well as shorelines on four of the five Great Lakes, Michigan is a recreational paradise. Resorts, cabins, camps, and parks line the shores of the lakes and rivers for year-round activities. In fact, Michigan is the leading state in the ownership of recreational boats, as well as in the sale of hunting and fishing licenses. There are also more than forty downhill ski areas, and four times that number of organized cross-country ski trails. Most of the best alpine slopes are in the northern part of the state, but there are also ski slopes near Detroit in the southwest. The northern two-thirds of the state also has excellent snow for snowmobiling. When it comes to outdoor fun, Michigan has something for everyone.

recover, under the leadership of Governor John Engler. Within a few short years, Michigan had risen to first in the nation in new business growth and first among all industrial states in economic development. Changes in the tax laws, privatization (changing to private ownership) of many state services, as well as welfare reform all contributed to the resurgence. The state was also successful in reforming its education programs.

At the end of the twentieth century, Michigan's business leaders continued to work toward expanding manufacturing and to attract more high-tech companies. No longer is there a major reliance on the auto industry as the mainstay of the state's economy.

More cars and trucks are built in Michigan than in any other state.

Other Things to Know About Michigan

- The city of Battle Creek makes more breakfast cereal than any other city in the world.
- Lake Michigan is the largest lake entirely in the United States.
- Grand Rapids is the site of the Gerald R. Ford Presidential Museum, which houses the papers and artifacts of the nation's thirty-eighth president.
- The Michigan park system is one of the largest in the country, with ninety-nine parks and recreation areas.
- Michigan State University won the NCAA national college basketball championship in the 1978–1979 season when the Spartans, led by Earvin "Magic" Johnson, defeated Larry Bird and Indiana State in the final game. Johnson and Bird both went on to championship, Hall of Fame careers in the National Basketball Association.

NATURAL RESOURCES: apples, beef cattle, blueberries, cherries, nursery products, hogs, horses, milk, eggs, dry beans, catfish, chub, whitefish, iron ore, bromine, gypsum, natural gas, petroleum, sand and gravel, stone, and peat

MANUFACTURED PRODUCTS: automobiles, transportation equipment, chemicals, electric and electronic equipment, processed food, furniture and fixtures, machinery, metals, and metal, rubber, and plastic products

WILDLIFE: black bear, great antlered moose, gray wolf, elk, deer, beaver, mink, red fox, porcupine, badger, and a variety of fish and birds

BATTLING OVER FORT DETROIT

The city of Detroit began as a fort on the Detroit River in 1701. It would prove to be a strategic location in several early wars. The British took the fort from the French on November 29, 1760, during the French and Indian War, and British conquests in the area displaced many Native Americans. In the spring of 1763, an alliance of Native Americans led by the Ottawa chief Pontiac rebelled against the British. Pontiac led an attack on Detroit. Though he didn't capture it, he kept it under siege for more than five months, withdrawing only when he learned the French had lost the war and ceded the territory to Great Britain. Then, during the War of 1812 (1812–15), there was much fighting along the United States–Canadian border. In August 1812, Detroit was surrendered to British forces, who had help from the Shawnee chief Tecumseh and his Native American forces. Finally, in September 1813, American naval forces defeated the British fleet in the Battle of Lake Erie. By regaining control of the water, the Americans forced the British to evacuate Detroit. It would be the last time that Detroit would be out of U.S. hands, and the fort would soon evolve into a major city.

State flower: Pink-and-white lady's slipper

MINNESOTA

State bird: Common loon

Minnesota, located in the north central United States, is the coldest of all states with the exception of Alaska. Canada borders it to the north, the Dakotas to the west, and Iowa to the south. Wisconsin and Lake Superior—one of the five Great Lakes—border to the east. The state's name comes from a Sioux word meaning "cloudy water," which referred to the light-colored clay suspended in a Minnesota River. Water continues to play a major role in the state. Minnesota has more than 15,000 lakes, providing a recreational bonanza. Though it is rich in minerals, farmland, and waterways, Minnesota has also become an important industrial state. In addition, it is home of the famous Twin Cities— Minneapolis, the state's largest city, and the state capital of Saint Paul.

Despite its extreme northern location, the largest part of the state—the Central Lowland—is made up of almost treeless plains, similar to the land throughout the Midwest. This makes it suitable for farming. The northern part of the state is more heavily forested. It is a paradise for hunting and fishing, and for tourism. At the same time, Minnesota has been the leading producer of iron ore in the United States since the 1880s.

As was the case with most states in the area, the early history of Minnesota was marked by conflicts between the British and French, as well as the Native Americans. Early French exploration began in the late seventeenth century. The object of this early exploration was to expand fur trading, which was mainly what took place in the area for many years. There was no settlement or major battle in the Minnesota Territory at the time of the French and Indian War (1754–63) or during the American Revolution (1775–83). But after the Louisiana Purchase in 1803, the United States had the entire Minnesota Territory under its flag.

Traders from the American Fur Company, owned by John Jacob Astor, made the first real encroachment into Minnesota early in the nineteenth century. The U.S. Army followed in 1819 and built a huge stone fortress called Fort Snelling at the spot where the Mississippi and Minnesota Rivers meet. Fort Snelling remained the pivotal point in the area until Saint Paul was established in 1840. Soon more settlers came, and the fur traders were joined by lumbermen. When neighboring Iowa and Wisconsin became states in 1846 and 1848, respectively, more people came into Minnesota. Between 1853 and 1857, the population of the Minnesota Territory grew from an estimated 40,000 to 150,000. Most of the newcomers were farmers who settled in the southern part of the territory.

With the population growing so rapidly, the pressure for statehood also grew. On May 11, 1858, Minnesota became the thirty-second state of the Union. But early statehood was not easy. In the first seven years, there was a depression, the Civil War (1861–65), and additional war with the Dakota people. The need for war supplies ended the economic hardship, and both the Civil War and war with the Native Americans ended at about the same time. Most of the Native Americans were driven into the Dakota Territory to the west, or north to Canada.

In the latter decades of the nineteenth century, Minnesota saw a huge influx of immigrants from Germany, Sweden, and Norway. Their labor helped in the growth of the farming, lumbering, and mining industries. By 1900, the state was almost completely settled, with the exception of some extreme northern areas. The population had grown to more than 1.75 million people.

Wheat farming reached its height in 1878, when about 70 percent of all the cultivated land was used for that purpose. The timber industry peaked in 1899. Mining continued to thrive. In 1894, John D. Rockefeller controlled the iron mining operations along the Mesabi mountain range. Rockefeller extended mining operations, and the state taxes on the industry paid for fine schools and other community services. Mining, however, was not always kind to the land.

Open-pit mining was used to extract the iron ore. Towns were located near the pits, but as the mines expanded, whole towns had

---

THE DANGERS OF LUMBERING

Lumbering was such an intense activity in Minnesota during the latter nineteenth century that its waste by-products often posed a grave danger. Tree stumps, abandoned piles of waste timber, and the stands of remaining trees often provided perfect conditions for fire. In 1894, a forest fire in Hinckley killed 413 people and caused $12 million in property damage. And in 1918, another fire destroyed Moose Lake and Cloquet, killing 559 people and causing property damage amounting to $25 million.

A MINNESOTAN MELTING POT

Throughout its history, America has been looked upon as a land of opportunity by peoples of other nations. In fact, as immigration increased, America became known as a melting pot, meaning that it was a mix of many different people from different lands. No state was more of a melting pot than Minnesota. The first foreign-born settlers in Minnesota were French Canadians, Swedes, Norwegians, Danes, Germans, and Irish. Later, by the end of the nineteenth century, Finns, Poles, Czechs, and Slovaks also settled in Minnesota. In the late twentieth century, there were people coming from the former Soviet Union, China, Vietnam, India, the Philippines, and Mexico.

The open-pit iron mine at Hibbing is the largest human-made hole in the world.

to be moved. One such town—Hibbing—was located on a rich deposit of ore. It was slowly moved to a new location between 1919 and 1946, with the original site becoming an enormous pit.

In the twentieth century, agriculture moved from a concentration on wheat to dairying, with an emphasis on producing butter and cheese. By the early 1990s, Minnesota ranked seventh among all states in farm income. Nearly three-fifths of the earnings came from the sale of livestock and livestock products, the rest from the sale of crops. The opening of the Saint Lawrence Seaway in 1959 made Duluth a world port. Ships could now travel through a series of locks, dams, and canals from Duluth and along the Saint Lawrence River, connecting the Great Lakes and flowing all the way to the Atlantic seaboard.

Minneapolis

Additional industry and a thriving tourist trade have also helped the state's economy. In 1987, the state had the nation's best high school graduation rate, 91.4 percent.

Other Things to Know About Minnesota

- The Mall of America, located in Bloomington, is the largest shopping mall in the United States. It has parking facilities for some 12,750 cars.
- One of the nation's most famous medical facilities, the Mayo Clinic, is located in Rochester.
- Sauk Centre was the boyhood home of novelist Sinclair Lewis, as well as the model for the fictional town of Gopher Prairie in his classic novel *Main Street.*
- The U.S. Hockey Hall of Fame is located in Eveleth.
- The boyhood home of famed aviator Charles A. Lindbergh is located in Little Falls. Lucky Lindy became a world hero when he flew his single-engine plane, the *Spirit of Saint Louis,* alone across the Atlantic Ocean in 1927.
- Minnesota politicians have often been on the national stage. Hubert H. Humphrey served in the U.S. Senate, was vice president under Lyndon Johnson, and was the Democratic nominee for president in 1968. Walter F. Mondale was also in the Senate, was vice president under Jimmy Carter, and was the Democratic nominee for president in 1984.

NATURAL RESOURCES: barley, beef cattle, corn, chickens, dry beans, eggs, hay, hogs, milk, oats, potatoes, soybeans, sugar beets, vegetables, wheat, wood, fish, iron ore, sand and gravel, and stone

MANUFACTURED PRODUCTS: chemicals, electric and electronic equipment, processed food, cheese, butter, dry milk, lumber, machinery, transportation equipment, printed materials, pulp, rubber, and wood, metal, plastic, paper, stone, clay, and glass products

WILDLIFE: black bear, timber wolf, moose, white-tailed deer, mule deer, red and gray fox, coyote, river otter, weasel, bobcat, and a large variety of birds, fish, and snakes

MISSISSIPPI

State bird: Mockingbird

Located in America's Deep South, within the Gulf Coastal Plain, Mississippi has often struggled to make the transition from the old ways of the nineteenth century into the modern world. One of the southern states where people depended on "king cotton" for their livelihoods, and slave labor to help provide it, Mississippians had to make many changes over the years. By the outset of the twenty-first century, however, African Americans were playing a major role in the state's political and economic development. At the same time, industry slowly began taking the place of agriculture, and all the people of the state looked toward better lives.

With the Gulf of Mexico directly to the south, Mississippi has a climate characterized by long, hot, humid summers and relatively mild winters. In the summer, days are generally hot and oppressive, with nighttime temperatures rarely falling below 70 degrees Fahrenheit. That leads to a long growing season and a climate conducive to growing cotton.

Though the Spanish and the French came to the Mississippi area earlier, the United States took possession of the land after the American Revolution (1775–83) and in 1798 created the Mississippi Territory. Natchez was made the territory's first capital, though the area had relatively few settlers. After the War of 1812 (1812–15), the territory was expanded to include what is now Alabama along with Mississippi. Alabama

became a separate territory in 1817, and in December of that year, Mississippi became the Union's twentieth state.

It was during this period that the first great migration of farmers began, most of them moving westward in search of land where they could grow cotton. From 1800 to 1820, the population grew from 7,600 to more than 75,000. Ten years later, there were more than 136,000 people living there. By this time, cotton was being planted in almost every part of the state, as more slaves were brought in to work the fields. As large plantations began springing up, a way of life was created based on cotton as the means to make money, and slaves to harvest the crops. By 1860, there were about 792,000 people in the state, but only 45 percent were white settlers. The remainder were the black slaves on whom the economy depended. The system made Mississippi the nation's leading producer of cotton.

So it was no surprise that at the outset of the Civil War (1861–65), Mississippi was one of the southern states to secede from the Union. About 80,000 Mississippians fought for the Confederacy, with some 25,000 of them dying before the war ended. In addition, when the Union Army captured Vicksburg in July 1863—after a long siege—it marked the last major Confederate stronghold on the Mississippi River. After that, the end of the war seemed a matter of time.

When the slaves were granted freedom after the war, Mississippi's economy was in turmoil. The Reconstruction period and beyond would be as hard or harder for Mississippi than any other state. There was a real reluctance to give former slaves the rights of freedom, and most had trouble earning a living on their own. The dependence on cotton remained, but even when production levels reached prewar levels, declining prices kept prosperity down. Small farmers went under. Sharecroppers and tenant farmers, working the land for others,

couldn't make enough money.

It didn't get much better in the early years of the twentieth century. There was very little industry to boost the economy during World War I (1914–18), and the Great Depression of the 1930s only increased the number of people living in poverty. Military bases set in Mississippi during World War II (1939–45) helped a bit, but then in the 1950s and 1960s, the state was the focus of America's great civil rights struggle. African Americans and their supporters began pushing harder for equality, a voice in government, and school desegregation. There was resistance from the establishment—and violence. Things began to improve slowly after 1965. By 1996, however, 10 of the 52 members of the Mississippi Senate were African American, as were 34 of the 122 members of the House of Representatives.

Farming also changed. In 1900, some 75 percent of all Mississippians earned a living on farms. By 1990, only 2.7 percent of the state's labor force worked on farms, while 22.7 percent worked in factories. In addition, while cotton still produces more money than any other single crop, the combination of soybeans, rice, poultry, and catfish produce twice as much income as cotton.

Industry has built on much of what was there. There are now plants for processing

Paddleboat steamers churn up the muddy waters of the Mississippi River.

A cotton field

poultry and catfish, industries based on wood products, and a growing furniture industry taking advantage of the large supply of lumber. Shipbuilding has grown on the Gulf Coast, while the cities are all developing pockets of heavy industry.

Yet Mississippi is still very much a rural state. By 1990, only 47 percent of its residents lived in cities. Jackson, the capital, is also the largest city, with a 1998 population of 192,923. The next largest city is Biloxi, which has fewer than 50,000 residents.

A ROUGH ROAD TO RECOVERY

The Civil Rights movement was as difficult a time in Mississippi as anywhere in the country. Old ways die hard, and at first every change from school desegregation to equal voting rights met resistance, sometimes with violent consequences. When James Meredith became the first African American to attend the University of Mississippi in 1962, federal troops had to be sent in to make sure the federal court order to desegregate was followed. A year later, in 1963, Medgar Evers, the state field secretary for the National Association for the Advancement of Colored People (NAACP), was shot dead in front of his Jackson home. Yet by 1965, all state schools had been integrated, and in 1969, Charles Evers, brother of the murdered Medgar, was elected mayor of Fayette; he was the first African American mayor in the history of the state. Change came hard, and with a price. But it did come.

Other Things to Know About Mississippi

- Mississippi has more tree farms than any other state, and is the largest producer of farmed catfish.
- The Old Spanish Fort at Pascagoula, originally built as a carpenter's or blacksmith's shack in 1718, is said to be the oldest existing building in the lower Mississippi Valley.
- Mississippi-born Jefferson Davis—a former U.S. senator and secretary of war—was elected the first president of the Confederate States of America at the outset of the Civil War.
- In the early 1990s, legalized gambling along the Mississippi River and the Gulf Coast increased the state's attraction for tourists.
- The Waterways Experiment Station near Jackson is the largest river model in the world, covering 210 acres. Using the station, engineers can predict when and where the Mississippi and its feeder rivers will overflow. They can then warn people living in the danger areas.

NATURAL RESOURCES: cotton, beef cattle, chickens, eggs, milk, rice, soybeans, vegetables, wood, menhaden, oysters, red snapper, shrimp, catfish, clay, natural gas, petroleum, and sand and gravel

MANUFACTURED PRODUCTS: chemicals, clothing, electrical equipment, processed food, furniture and fixtures, lumber, machinery, transportation equipment, guitar amplifiers, and wood, paper, and petroleum products

WILDLIFE: white-tailed deer, fox, weasel, nutria, alligator, turtle, both poisonous and non-poisonous snakes, and a large variety of birds and fish

State flower: Hawthorn

MISSOURI

State bird: Bluebird

At the time it became the Union's twenty-forth state in 1821, Missouri was considered to be on the young nation's western frontier. Because it became a stepping-off point for brave pioneers who wanted to make their homes in largely uncharted territory in Oregon and California, Missouri became known as the "Gateway to the West." That seems odd now, because Missouri is located in the geographic heart of the nation. It is bordered on the north by Iowa, on the west by Nebraska, Kansas, and Oklahoma, on the south by Arkansas, and on the east by the Mississippi River, which separates it from Tennessee, Kentucky, and Illinois. It is no wonder that Missouri has often been caught in conflicts between north and south, east and west.

In fact, Missouri has retained elements from all its surrounding regions. It remains a major agricultural state, while also serving as one of the most important manufacturing states in the Midwest. It has the wheat and cornfields of the Midwest, cotton fields of the South, grazing cattle as in the West, and a manufacturing heritage from the East. All of that, not unexpectedly, makes for an interesting history.

Missouri was a state bitterly divided during the Civil War (1861–65). It was the home of legendary outlaws Frank and Jesse James. Writer Mark Twain was born there, as was the World War I (1914–18) hero General John J. Pershing. Harry S. Truman, the thirty-third president of the United States, was also a native Missourian. The history of the "Gateway to the West" offers something for everyone.

French explorers came down the Mississippi River through Missouri in 1673. The first permanent settlement was made by the French in 1750. They had come to Missouri to mine the lead deposits found there. In 1764, a village was erected on the present site of Saint Louis. By 1770, the Spanish had taken over the area. The United States did not take full control of the region until the Louisiana Purchase of 1803. By that time, more than 10,000 people were living in the Missouri area.

In June 1812, the Missouri Territory was created from the Louisiana Territory, with borders similar to those of the present state. Three years later—when the War of 1812 (1812–15) ended—immigrants came to the territory at a very fast pace. Many were from the South and brought their slaves with them. By 1820, the population had risen to 70,000, with lead mining and trapping the main sources of revenue. Missouri was a rough place to live then, with a lot of gambling, drinking, and brawling.

Because the nation was already becoming embroiled in the controversy about the ethics of slavery, the Missouri Compromise was passed by Congress in 1820. It was intended to keep the balance between free and slave states. Missouri would be allowed to enter the union as a slave state, while Maine gained entry as a free state. That led to Missouri becoming the twenty-fourth state on August 10, 1821.

The state continued to grow rapidly. By 1860, there were 1.2 million people living in Missouri. Many of them would be bitterly divided when the Civil War (1861–65) began the next year. Even before the war started, the Kansas-Missouri border was a battleground between pro- and antislavery groups. Despite a great deal of opposition, Missouri opted to remain on the Union side once the war began. During the war, some 110,000 Missourians fought with the Union forces, while 40,000 sided with the Confederates. It was surely a state divided.

After the war, even more people came. Between 1870 and 1900, Missouri was fifth in population among all the states. Yet farmers continued to struggle and the many immigrants flocking to Saint Louis flooded the labor market and caused wages to fall. But during this period, the growth of the railroad laid the groundwork for a financial comeback.

As did many other states, Missouri prospered during World War I (1914–18) and the economy continue to grow during the 1920s. The Great Depression of the 1930s slowed everything, with the U.S. entry in World War II (1939–45), in 1941, putting people back to work. In the 1950s and 1960s, Missouri dealt with issues of school desegregation, then a gradual change from manufacturing to the service sector as the state's chief employer. People continued to move from rural to urban areas, with Kansas City and Saint Louis growing and adding suburbs in the surrounding countryside.

At the outset of the twenty-first century, Missouri faces the same challenges as much of the rest of the nation—the rising cost of higher education; downsizing of large industrial corporations; low wages in the service area; lack of adequate child care; and growing crime in the cities. However, Missouri still has the second highest number of farms and remains a leading agricultural state. It is also one of the leading manufacturing states west of the Mississippi, with Saint Louis as the focal point for river transportation and the nation's largest inland river port.

DID YOU KNOW . . .
Gateway Arch in Saint Louis is the tallest monument in the United States, standing 630 feet high.

THE PONY EXPRESS

Missouri was not only the Gateway to the West for pioneers; for a short period of time in the nineteenth century, it was the Gateway to the West—for mail delivery! The Pony Express began on April 3, 1860, with a series of riders on horseback carrying mail from Saint Joseph, Missouri, to Sacramento, California. They rode nearly 2,000 miles in ten days, with rest stations about 25 miles apart. Riders were usually lightweight young men, often teenagers. They had special saddlebags that could be changed quickly from one horse to another at the change stations. The service employed eighty riders, and between 400 and 500 horses. Despite the danger of the trip, only one mail delivery was ever lost.

THE CARDINALS, A GREAT BASEBALL TRADITION

Saint Louis has a long and glorious baseball tradition. The Cardinals—an old National League franchise—have been to the World Series fifteen times, and have won nine championships. Only the New York Yankees have had more long-term success. In 1998, the eyes of the baseball world and much of America again focused on the Cardinals, as first baseman Mark McGwire chased and broke one of baseball's most cherished records. McGwire slammed a total of 70 home runs, racing past the old record of 61, set by the Yankees' Roger Maris in 1961. McGwire's record didn't last long. The Giants' Barry Bonds broke it by clubbing 73 homers in 2001.

Council Bluff Lake is the largest of the lakes in Mark Twain National Forest.

Other Things to Know About Missouri

- The first ice cream cone was sold at the World's Fair in Saint Louis, in 1904.
- The Southeastern Lowland region of Missouri has had some of the biggest earthquakes in U.S. history. A pair of quakes in 1811 and 1812 were both above 8 on the Richter scale. They were so strong that they caused some lands to sink and others to rise, and they altered the course of the Mississippi River.
- Missouri is first in the nation in the production of lead.
- The Harry S. Truman Home and the Truman Library and Museum, both in Independence, feature exhibits about the life and career of the nation's thirty-third president.
- Though many were skirmishes with roving bands of guerillas, more than 1,000 battles and clashes took place in Missouri during the Civil War.

NATURAL RESOURCES: beef cattle, corn, cotton, hay, hogs, milk, rice, sorghum, soybeans, wheat, coal, iron ore, lead, stone, and zinc

MANUFACTURED PRODUCTS: chemicals, processed food, electric and electronic equipment, machinery, metal products, transportation equipment, and printed materials

WILDLIFE: deer, opossum, raccoon, skunk, hawk, quail, wild turkey, variety of small birds, bass, pike, catfish, buffalo fish, sturgeon, and rattlesnake and copperhead snake

State flower: Bitterroot

MONTANA

State bird: Western meadowlark

The fourth largest state in the Union (after Alaska, Texas, and California), Montana ranks just forty-fourth in population, with fewer than one million people. Not surprisingly, Montana still has acres upon acres of untamed wilderness. It contains a section of Yellowstone National Park as well as the entire Glacier National Park. There are mountains, multitudes of hiking trails, lakes loaded with fish, and ski resorts—all of which make Montana the perfect getaway place for those who love the great outdoors.

With Canada located to the north, the Dakotas to the east, Wyoming to the south, and Idaho to the west, Montana not only has forested mountain ranges, but also a section of the Great Plains in the eastern part of the state. Since there are abundant natural resources as well as plains for farmland, it seems, at first, that Montana should have become more densely settled. However, the climate is so extreme that there can be temperatures well below zero degrees Fahrenheit in winter as well as severe summer hailstorms. Montana may be a great place to visit, but it isn't always easy to live there.

Though Europeans explored the Montana territory early in the eighteenth century, it wasn't until the Louisiana Purchase of 1803 that much of the area was charted. Explorers brought back stories of a land full of beaver and other fur-bearing animals. By 1807, several fur-trading companies were competing for business, and the first trading post was established on the Bighorn

River. When gold was discovered in 1862, the prospectors started coming. Boomtowns sprang up. Outlaws soon followed, looking to steal a booty in gold. Vigilante groups were formed to combat the outlaws, making Montana a very rough and dangerous place to be.

During these years, Montana was part of seven different U.S. territories. It wasn't until May 1864 that Montana was made a territory unto itself, with its own elected legislature. With all these changes, there continued to be clashes between whites and Native Americans. In 1874, gold was discovered within the boundaries of the Sioux reservation in the Black Hills. That led to one of the infamous battles in American history. On June 25, 1876, Sioux and Cheyenne forces, under Sitting Bull and Crazy Horse, defeated U.S. troops under the command of General George Armstrong Custer. In a battle still debated to this day, Custer's troops were all killed. It was the last major Native American victory. Crazy Horse surrendered in 1877, and Sitting Bull surrendered in 1881.

Mining and the raising of livestock were key to the territory's economy. But there were problems between various mining groups, and cattle ranchers often fought with sheepherders. Nothing came easily. Overgrazing and extreme weather conditions led to the death of some 60 percent of the cattle in 1886. The cattle range was finally fenced at the end of the nineteenth century, and the traditional cattle drives from Texas to Montana ended.

Statehood came on November 8, 1889, making Montana the forty-first state admitted to the Union. Helena was the capital of the new state, which was finally starting to grow. From 1880 to 1890, the population increased from about 40,000 to 143,00. By 1900, there were almost 243,000 residents. The completion of the railroads made it easier for people to live and work in the state. Farmers began growing wheat, and with above-average rainfall from 1909 to 1916, production flourished. World War I (1914–18) further increased demand, and

THE PHENOMENON OF BOOMTOWNS

When the Montana gold rush began in earnest in 1862, hundreds of prospectors, miners, and fortune seekers flocked to the area. Whenever there were rumors of a gold strike, people came and quickly began to build a town. Known as boomtowns for the speed with which they were built, grew, and prospered, they often declined just as quickly when the gold played out. Bannack—the first of the boomtowns—had a population of about 500 in 1862. By 1864, there were 1,000 people living there, and the name was changed to Bannack City. Virginia City was founded in 1863 and grew to have a population of 10,000 people. Helena was founded at Last Chance Gulch after gold was discovered in 1864. The original boomtowns were often characterized by makeshift dwellings and a lawless element. In the 1860s, they were very dangerous places to live.

the farmers prospered. But once again the weather dealt a crippling blow. A severe drought in 1917 caused dust-bowl conditions. Hordes of grasshoppers followed and devoured the remaining crops. Many farms soon went out of business.

The annual Crow Fair is held outside of Billings each August.

THE MONTANA WILDERNESS

In an effort to preserve its beautiful wilderness, the state of Montana has set aside several areas to ensure that the character of the land is preserved. Even motor vehicles are prohibited in these areas, with visitors traveling by packhorse or on foot. Those willing to rough it, however, can see some of the most spectacular scenery in the country. The Bob Marshall Wilderness—combined with the Great Bear and Scapegoat wilderness areas—adds up to an area of more than 1.5 million acres. In some of these areas, wildlife is protected, to further preserve the wilderness as it has existed for thousands of years.

During the Great Depression of the 1930s, prices dropped. Mining suffered from foreign competition, and drought plagued the farmers. The New Deal legislation of the 1930s instituted water-control and irrigation systems, the most important being the construction of the Fort Peck Dam on the Missouri River.

It was only after World War II (1939–45) that Montana once again began to edge toward prosperity. The postwar building boom brought Montana's lumber industry to life. Oil production also increased after the war. By the 1960s, natural gas had also become a major product, and tourism began to boom. Today, the state is taking full advantage of its many natural resources to bring people and money into Montana.

Today, agriculture, mining, timber processing, and tourism remain the major industries. Billings is the state's largest city, but still has fewer than 100,000 residents. In many areas, it is the wide-open spaces that prevail. While more people may eventually settle in Montana, it remains one of America's last unspoiled places and a great place to visit.

Other Things to Know About Montana

- In some years, as much as 300 inches of snow can fall in the mountains in the western part of the state.
- Because of the harsh and changing weather, Montana's highways are difficult and expensive to maintain. Freezing and thawing in the winter months continually cause bad breaks and potholes in highway surfaces.
- The Big Hole National Battlefield, near Wisdom, marks the site where U.S. troops were defeated by Chief Joseph and the Nez Perce on August 9, 1877. The Nez Perce then sought refuge in Canada.
- Women in Montana had civil rights earlier than women in most of the rest of the country. Beginning in 1869, the territorial government permitted women to vote in some local and school elections. In 1916, Jeannette Rankin became the first woman elected to the U.S. House of Representatives.
- At Medicine Rocks are sandstone buttes that have been formed into strange shapes by the forces of wind and rain.
- *Montana* is a Spanish word meaning "mountain."

NATURAL RESOURCES: beef cattle, sheep, barley, hay, wheat, sugar beets, coal, copper, gold, gemstones, natural gas, zinc, silver, platinum-palladium, and petroleum

MANUFACTURED PRODUCTS: processed food, chemicals, lumber, metals, wool, and petroleum, wood, and coal products

WILDLIFE: white-tailed deer, mule deer, Rocky Mountain elk, black bear, grizzly bear, antelope, Rocky Mountain bighorn sheep, mountain goat, moose, caribou, mountain lion, bison, beaver, bobcat, lynx, wolverine, a large variety of birds, including the bald eagle, golden eagle, and Swainson's hawk, as well as a large variety of fish

NEBRASKA

State bird: Western meadowlark

Another state in America's heartland is Nebraska, located midway between the Atlantic and Pacific Oceans. It is bordered by South Dakota, Kansas, Iowa, Missouri, Wyoming, and Colorado and is almost rectangular in shape, with four-fifths of the land part of the Great Plains. Since the middle of the nineteenth century, Nebraska's economy has been based almost solely on agriculture. This includes the raising of livestock, and the growing of corn (much of which is used for livestock feed) and wheat.

Until modern irrigation methods were instituted in the second half of the twentieth century, Nebraskans had to hope for good weather to have a successful year. When there were deviations—such as prolonged drought—the people and the economy suffered. Even when the state began to industrialize and move into the manufacturing sector, it was agriculture that got them started. Food processing (led by meatpacking) accounted for about one-quarter of the state's industrial income by the early 1990s.

Nebraska was another of the central Plains states that originally served as a way station for settlers traveling west in the mid-nineteenth century. The United States took over the region with the Louisiana Purchase of 1803. In 1820, explorer Stephen H. Long followed the Platte River through much of the area. He reported later that the Great Plains consisted of a huge desert and endorsed Zebulon Pike's earlier opinion that white settlement should be confined to lands east of the Mississippi River.

Because of Long's report, the federal government began relocating Native Americans to lands west of the Mississippi, including present-day Nebraska. At that time, the lands became known as Indian Territory. Soon, however, the lands were becoming more important to whites. Many passed through the area on their way west, and some settlers and traders began to stay.

The passing of the Kansas-Nebraska Act in 1854 created the territories of Kansas and Nebraska and opened much of the area to legal white settlement. The early settlements were located along the Missouri River in the east as well as on the Platte River, which ran east to west. Because the settlers in Nebraska had little interest in establishing slavery, the territory was free of battle during the Civil War (1861–65). Then, on March 1, 1867, Nebraska became the thirty-seventh state admitted to the Union. The village of Lancaster, located on the banks of the Salt Creek, was renamed Lincoln and made the state capital.

SOD HOUSES

There were so few trees in Nebraska that early settlers had to build houses from sod cut into bricks. Each block of sod had the roots from grasses in it, which held the sod together. Once the homes were built, settlers began planting trees for shade, fruit, and lumber. In 1872, newspaper publisher J. Sterling Morton took things a step further. He asked leaders of the new state to set aside a special day for tree planting. Nebraska now has the only national forest completely planted by human beings, proving that a forest can grow on the Plains. The trees planted so long ago stop the winds from blowing the dry earth away. People all over the United States now plant trees on Arbor Day, following the example of J. Sterling Morton.

After the Civil War, Nebraska grew rapidly. Moving from a population of less than 30,000 in 1860, the state would be closing in on the one-million mark by 1890. The completion of the Union Pacific Railroad in 1869 helped greatly. The Burlington Railroad followed soon afterward, and the two rail lines were granted more than seven-eighths of the nearly 17 percent of Nebraska's land that was given to the railroads by the federal government. The two lines then sold parcels to settlers at low prices, to help the population increase and to promote agriculture. Products could now be shipped by rail to provide increased profits for all.

But with wood and water scarce in most of the state, settlers didn't have it easy. They often had to cut bricks of sod from the ground to build houses. They often had to dig down more than 300 feet before they hit water for wells. Farmers were susceptible to the weather, especially droughts. In dry years, crops were poor, and the people suffered. The situation was finally improved when modern irrigation methods were implemented in the second half of the twentieth century.

The years during World War I (1914–18) brought prosperity to the state. The increased demand for food and the luck of bountiful rains caused even more land to be brought under cultivation. Crop prices fell, however, during the 1920s and crashed during the Great Depression of the 1930s. In fact, in 1932, crop prices fell to the lowest

Scout's Rest Ranch at North Platte was the home of Buffalo Bill Cody and the training ground for his famous Wild West Show.

point in state history. Farm foreclosures increased, showing once again how dependent the state's economy was on agriculture.

Between 1945 and 1990, the amount of irrigated land increased from 900,000 acres to almost 8 million acres. The federal government also began subsidizing farms to keep the state's economy strong. There was yet another crisis in the 1980s, when many farmers couldn't afford the large loans needed to modernize and were driven into bankruptcy. Only the metropolitan areas of Omaha and Lincoln escaped the effects of the crisis.

Both the state and federal governments continue to try to help the farmer and the agricultural economy. In the 1990s, the cost of education and health insurance continued to rise, with property taxes remaining high. The rural population is now declining, but smaller companies across the state are helping the economy.

RED CLOUD'S WAR

By 1854, nearly all the lands in eastern Nebraska had been ceded to whites, while the Sioux and Cheyenne remained in control of the western lands. In the early 1860s, the U.S. Army decided to open the Bozeman Trail, which led to the Montana gold fields and crossed an important Oglala Sioux hunting ground. When Red Cloud, an Oglala, became leader of a large group of Sioux and Cheyenne in 1866, he began fighting the construction of three army forts that would protect travelers on the Bozeman Trail. For more than two years, Red Cloud fought the army, until the Treaty of Fort Laramie was signed in 1869. Outwardly, it appeared as if the United States would abandon the Bozeman Trail. But those who drew up the treaty were deceitful; the treaty contained a provision that would relocate the Sioux from Nebraska to a reservation in what is now South Dakota. Many Sioux refused to move and continued fighting. Red Cloud visited Washington and was possibly overwhelmed by the large numbers of whites. Realizing he couldn't win, he resigned himself to life as a reservation chief.

Industries such as telecommunications, insurance, health care, and tourism are bolstering the economy at the turn of the century. Ironically, farm life—so important to the state and so difficult 150 years ago—remains difficult today.

Prairie dogs

Other Things to Know About Nebraska

- Ruts made by the wagon wheels of pioneer families more than 100 years ago can still be seen in the dirt beside some roads
- Nebraska is the only state whose nickname, the Cornhusker State, comes from a college football team—the University of Nebraska Cornhuskers.
- In 1894, the editor of the Nebraska *World-Herald* newspaper was William Jennings Bryan, who would run for president of the United States on three different occasions.
- Novelist Willa Cather grew up on a farm near Red Cloud, and her earliest novels were inspired by life on the Nebraska prairie.
- Two top World War I generals, John J. Pershing and Charles G. Dawes, both came from Lincoln, Nebraska.

NATURAL RESOURCES: beef cattle, corn, wheat, hay, sorghum, soybeans, sugar beets, hogs, great northern beans, natural gas, petroleum, and sand and gravel

MANUFACTURED PRODUCTS: chemicals, processed food, electric and electronic equipment, instruments, machinery, metals and metal products, transportation equipment, and meatpacking

WILDLIFE: bison, mule deer, white-tailed deer, pronghorn, coyote, prairie dog, beaver, pheasant, quail, sharp-tailed grouse, prairie chicken, wild turkey, and a variety of fish

State flower: Sagebrush

NEVADA

State bird: Mountain bluebird

When most people think of Nevada, they think of Las Vegas, the neon-lit city in the desert that's alive twenty-four hours a day with gambling casinos, resort hotels, famous entertainers, and throngs of tourists. But Nevada can also be described as a stark and arid land. It receives the least rain of all the states, and the skies are usually clear, with bright sunshine and low humidity. Despite the crowds in Las Vegas, Nevada is the third least densely populated state in the nation, behind only Alaska and Wyoming.

The state—whose name was taken from the Sierra Nevada mountain range (*nevada* is Spanish for "snow covered")—sits just east of California. Nevada is made up mostly of mountains and desert, which explains why so much of the state is sparsely populated. In fact, there was no permanent settlement in Nevada until 1850. Yet just fourteen years later, in 1864, Nevada became the Union's thirty-sixth state, the only state admitted while the Civil War (1861–65) was still raging in the eastern half of the country.

Because of its location, Nevada was not explored by Europeans as early as many other states. There was some exploration after 1826, but the first thorough exploration of the Great Basin (which lies between the Sierra Nevada mountains of California and the Wasatch Range of Utah), was done by John Charles Frémont, beginning in 1843. The information he gathered helped settlers to cross the Great Basin on their way to

California. But up to that time, no one (except for various Native American tribes) had attempted to settle in Nevada.

Two events changed all that. At the end of the U.S.-Mexican War (1846–48), the United States acquired Nevada, as well as California, Arizona, Utah, and parts of New Mexico, Colorado, and Wyoming. This made it much easier to travel west. That same year, gold was discovered in California. That made many more people *want* to travel west. In 1850, the government created the Utah Territory, which included much of present-day Nevada. The first permanent settlement was created that same year, when a trading post was built on the site of present-day Genoa.

Though there weren't many settlers in the territory, they petitioned for their own territorial government in 1857 and again in 1859. In March 1861, a bill was signed creating the Territory of Nevada. One reason that it was passed was the discovery of both gold and silver at the Comstock Lode in 1859. Finally, in October 1864, Nevada became the thirty-sixth state. With the Civil War still raging, President Abraham Lincoln saw Nevada's statehood as additional support for the Thirteenth Amendment to the Constitution, which outlawed slavery. Statehood also provided more voters to support Lincoln in the upcoming presidential election.

From 1860 to 1910, Nevada's economy was tied to a pair of mining booms, which were separated by a twenty-year depression, from 1880 to 1900. The Comstock Lode discovery brought thousands of people to the area, including a large number of immigrants. Chinese immigrants helped build the railroads, Italians and Swiss worked in the smelters (where ore was melted), and the Irish worked deep in the mines. French Canadians were in the lumber trade, Germans farmed, and Basques and Scots tended sheep.

Red Rock Canyon National Conservation Area

The wealth from the Comstock Lode helped build hotels, banks, foundries, and railroads. The Comstock Lode played out by 1880 and was followed by twenty difficult years, until rich silver ore was discovered at Tonopah, in southwestern Nevada. Later, more silver was found at other locations, and the resulting boom bolstered the economy right into the twentieth century.

Reno became a wide-open frontier town after World War I (1914–18), with illegal gambling and the sale of alcoholic beverages—then also illegal by Constitutional amendment—permitted everywhere. Life was fast and loose in Reno, and soon spilled over to the small railroad town of Las Vegas. The gambling and liquor business continued to grow, even in the Great Depression. In 1931 (the same year construction began on the Hoover Dam), gambling was legalized.

It was after the end of World War II (1939–45) that the gambling and entertainment industries in Reno and Las Vegas really began to expand. The opening of the huge Flamingo Hotel in 1947 (which was in large part the brainchild of the gangster Benjamin "Bugsy" Siegel) changed the face of gambling in Las Vegas. By 1951, there were five large hotel-resort casinos operating just outside Vegas, and the city was often called "the entertainment capital of the world."

Today, the population of Nevada is concentrated along the California border, with some 75 percent living in or near Las Vegas. It is the fastest-growing state in the country.

HOOVER DAM

In 1931, the U.S. government funded the Boulder Canyon project, to build a huge dam in the Black Canyon on the Colorado River in Nevada, on the border of Arizona. Construction would take five years. Upon completion, Boulder Dam (the name had been changed from Hoover Dam) was the world's tallest dam, rising 726 feet above the bed of the Colorado River. The gravity-arch structure encompassed many innovations in large-dam building that were used for the first time. Upon completion, it provided flood control, hydroelectric power, and drinking and irrigation water to regions as far away as southern California. The dam's name was changed back to Hoover (after President Herbert Hoover) in 1947. Lake Mead—the reservoir formed behind the dam—is one of the largest artificially created bodies of water in the world, covering 233 square miles, with a shoreline of 550 miles.

But the gaming economy has also caused problems, such as increased crime, air pollution, divorce, alcoholism, drug use, gang activity, and

Las Vegas

suicide. Yet people continue to flock to this oasis in the desert. In addition to gambling and entertainment, gold mining in eastern Nevada, near Elko, has made Nevada one of the top producers of gold in the world.

Other Things to Know About Nevada

- Nevada has the most wild horses of any state.
- More than $300 million in gold and silver were taken out of the Comstock Lode between 1860 and 1880.
- Lake Tahoe, in the Sierra Nevada mountains (and partially in California), has become a favorite resort stop for tourists. It has everything from water sports to skiing.
- Because of the dry conditions and lack of vegetation, ranches in Nevada are huge so that livestock can find enough food on which to graze. Only Arizona and Wyoming have ranges that are— on average—larger than Nevada's.
- Tourism is now Nevada's most important economic industry.
- Famed American writer Mark Twain was a reporter and editor of the Nevada *Territorial Enterprise* in the 1860s. Twain's book, *Roughing It*, published in 1872, described his experiences in Nevada.
- Tourists can visit old mining camps such as Virginia City, as well as a number of ghost towns left behind after the state's first gold rush.
- Because Nevada is the only western state where most kinds of gambling are legal, a steady stream of tourists comes to Las Vegas in the hope of striking it rich.
- While Las Vegas and Reno are the state's biggest cities by far, the state capital is Carson City, which has a population of about 50,000 people.

NATURAL RESOURCES: beef cattle, greenery and nursery products, hay, milk, potatoes, gold, silver, barite, copper, diatomite, gypsum, lime, lithium, mercury, and petroleum

MANUFACTURED PRODUCTS: electric and electronic equipment, processed food, instruments, machinery, printed materials, rubber, plastics, and metal, stone, clay, and glass products

WILDLIFE: bighorn sheep, mule deer, pronghorn antelope, fox, beaver, muskrat, bobcat, lynx, cougar, porcupine, coyote, badger, lizard, desert tortoise, diamondback and sidewinder rattlesnake, scorpion, tarantula, Gila monster, and a variety of game birds and fish

State flower: Purple lilac

NEW HAMPSHIRE

State bird: Purple finch

Situated in the northeastern part of the country, New Hampshire is the seventh smallest and one of the oldest states in the Union, having been settled just three years after the landing of the Pilgrims at Plymouth, Massachusetts, in 1620. The state was given its name by Captain John Mason, an early settler, who named it after the county of Hampshire in Great Britain, where he spent part of his youth. This triangle-shaped state is bordered by Canada to the north and Massachusetts to the south, with Vermont to the west and Maine and the Atlantic Ocean to the east. New Hampshire was one of the original thirteen colonies

New Hampshire's climate is characterized by cool summers and long, cold winters. The presidential mountain range in the north central part of the state has some of the most severe winters in the eastern United States. In fact, the highest wind velocity on record, a frightening 231 miles per hour, was recorded on Mount Washington. Despite a short growing season and relatively infertile, stony soil, the first settlers lived by farming and agriculture.

The first English settlement was started in 1623 by a Scotsman, David Thomson, at Odiorne's Point. Thomson and his small group set up a few farms and a trading post. Around 1630, the settlers moved to the site of present-day Portsmouth. In 1638, both Exeter and Hampton were settled. There was also an earlier settlement at Dover. These four remained the only permanent settlements in New Hampshire until 1673.

At first, the settlers and Native Americans got along. The Native Americans helped the settlers learn to farm, and eventually other settlers became craftsmen—cabinetmakers, ironworkers, bricklayers, clockmakers, or those who fashioned things from pewter. Lumbering and shipbuilding were two early industries that began to grow in the area.

But as the number of whites increased, so did tensions with the Native Americans. The Europeans brought in livestock, which often trampled the Native Americans' crops. Soon there were disputes over hunting and fishing grounds. After a half century of friendship, the relationship changed. From about 1689 to 1760, New Hampshire was a battleground not only between France and England for control of North America, but also between Native Americans and English settlers. After a number of bloody battles and skirmishes, most of the surviving native peoples left the

New Hampshire region after the 1720s.

Though there were no battles fought in New Hampshire during the American Revolution (1775–83), the colony made a major contribution to the war effort. New Hampshire Minutemen fought the British from the start. Later, three regiments from New Hampshire joined the war effort, while about 100 privateers (privately owned armed vessels) sailed out of Portsmouth Harbor to attack British ships. After the war, New Hampshire became the ninth state to ratify the Constitution of the United States, voting yes on June 21, 1788.

At the beginning of the nineteenth century, most of New Hampshire was prospering. Farming continued to be a prime source of revenue, as were fishing, commerce, and lumber. Waterpower and the development of the railroads helped create industrial centers in Portsmouth, Nashua, Concord, Dover, and Manchester.

New Hampshire was an ardent supporter of the Union during the Civil War (1861–65). Yet during and after the war, the population of the state decreased, as many farm families left to seek more fertile soils and government land grants in the West. Still, manufacturing continued, and by the end of the century, the state was a leading producer of shoes, textiles, and wood products, with the majority of the population living in the cities.

Early in the twentieth century, more immigrants came into the state, providing labor for industry. At the same time, new and elegant hotels brought an influx of wealthy tourists to the White Mountains, making tourism a profitable industry as well. But there were hard times after World War I (1914–18) ended, and more economic downturns occurred during the Great Depression of the 1930s. As was the case in other states, the demands on industry caused by World War II (1939–45) helped to turn the economy around. Eighty-two submarines were launched from the Portsmouth Navy Yard alone, between 1940 and 1945.

More new businesses started during the early and mid-1950s, as the state's popula-

There are many well-preserved eighteenth-century towns throughout New Hampshire, many of which still have white wooden churches, public greens or commons, and early American homes.

tion began growing. Between 1950 and 1990, it increased from 533,000 to more than one million. Today, New Hampshire continues to move toward taking its place in the modern world of high technology and development, while trying to retain the characteristics of a rural tradition that goes back to the country's beginnings. It remains a typical Yankee state, with beautiful land, lakes, mountains, and places to visit and vacation.

GIVE US OUR SHIPS

As an early English colony in America, New Hampshire had natural resources that its ruling country, Great Britain, coveted. Not the least of these was its lumber, which the British saw as a great resource for building the ships it used to dominate the seas and colonize distant parts of the world. New Hampshire lumber was soon being used to create boards, staves, and masts that were shipped to England. White pine was especially suitable for the making of masts. During the winter, a representative of the king of England would come to New Hampshire and mark trees that would be made into masts. The trees were then cut, hauled over the snow to the river, and floated to the sea. The term *mast road* is still used in New Hampshire for the part of several modern roads that were once the trails along which the masts were dragged.

Other Things to Know About New Hampshire

- The first town-supported, free public library in the United States opened in New Hampshire in 1833.
- Mount Washington is the highest mountain in the northeast, at 6,288 feet.
- New Hampshire was the first colony to set up its own government, six months before the Declaration of Independence was signed.
- New Hampshire has more than 1,300 lakes and ponds, the largest of which is Lake Winnipesaukee, which is seventy-two square miles in size.
- Manchester, the state's largest city, has barely more than 100,000 residents.

NATURAL RESOURCES: lumber, hay, maple syrup, milk, fruits and vegetables, lobster, cod, pollock, shrimp, clay, sand and gravel, stone, and granite

MANUFACTURED PRODUCTS: lumber, electric and electronic equipment, instruments, machinery, metal, paper, printed materials, rubber, and wood, metal, plastic, and paper products

WILDLIFE: black bear, moose, white-tailed deer, fox, muskrat, mink, bobcat, beaver, porcupine, a variety of birds, and an abundance of fish

Dartmouth College

FESTIVALS OF FUN

New Hampshire is filled with annual festivals that attract tourists. The most famous of the winter festivals is at Dartmouth College in Hanover, where craftsmen construct (among other things) elaborate ice sculptures. Music festivals include the All-State Music Festival in April, the annual Stark Fiddlers' Contest in June, and the Pemi Valley Bluegrass Festival in Compton each August. There is the Sheep and Wool Festival each May in New Boston, and a crafts fair by the League of New Hampshire Craftsmen at Mount Sunapee in August. The High Games at Loon Mountain in Lincoln are a September staple, while antique and classic automobiles are featured at the Fall Foliage Tour in Charlestown every October.

State flower: Purple violet

NEW JERSEY

State bird: Eastern goldfinch

The third state to ratify the Constitution of the United States, on December 18, 1787, New Jersey has been at the hub of the country's activities since the beginning. It is the fifth smallest state in the Union, but the most densely populated of them all. Located between New York City and Philadelphia, New Jersey is in the heart of a highly urbanized area called a "megalopolis." The state is in the forefront of industrial research and development, with many residents commuting to work in the nearby large cities. Yet with all this activity, there are still a few remaining wilderness areas, such as the mountains in the northwest and the sparsely settled southern tidelands. And the longtime nickname of New Jersey continues to be The Garden State.

A Middle Atlantic state with Pennsylvania located to the west, the Hudson River separating it from New York to the north and northeast, a long eastern coast along the Atlantic Ocean, and the Delaware Bay and Delaware River separating it from Delaware to the south and southwest, New Jersey has a varied climate that can range from hot and humid tropical air in summer to heavy snowfalls in winter. In addition, because it is along the Atlantic seaboard, parts of the state are subjected to heavy rains and occasionally hurricane conditions. Yet the early colonists who came to New Jersey in the seventeenth century saw the area as a garden paradise, with an agricultural bounty for all.

The Italian navigator Giovanni da Verrazzano explored and charted the New Jersey coast in 1524, but it wasn't until 1620 that a trading post was established at Bergen by the Dutch, and settlement began. The area was called New Netherland, but in 1664 the Dutch surrendered it to the English, who renamed it New Jersey—for the island of Jersey in the English Channel.

When Europeans first arrived, the area was inhabited by Native Americans, who were primarily peaceful farmers. Though the treatment of Native Americans was better in New Jersey than it would be in other parts of the country, many died from diseases that whites brought with them, and others were forced from their homes as the settlers wanted more land. Though there was little violence, most of the Native Americans were gone from New Jersey by about 1800.

In 1702, New Jersey was united as a royal colony, and a tradition of self-government was established. At that time, there were about 14,000 people living in New Jersey. More people began coming, and on the eve of the American Revolution (1775–83), some 120,000 people lived there. Many of the new-comers were immigrants of diverse back-grounds from New York and Philadelphia.

After the war, New Jersey became the third state to ratify the Constitution, and it continued to grow. Roads, canals, and finally the railroad began making it easier for peo-ple to travel and goods to be shipped. Toward the middle of the nineteeth century, New Jersey small towns were becoming industrial centers, taking advantage of the strategic location between New York City and Philadelphia. Though no battles were fought in New Jersey during the Civil War (1861–65), the state put more than 88,000 men in uniform, vigorously opposing the secession of the southern states.

New Jersey prospered both during and after the war, as many new industries and businesses flocked to the state. There was also an influx of wealthy industrialists who commuted to New York and Philadelphia to work, but chose to live in large homes in such places as Somerset, Morris, Monmouth, and Essex counties. The factory workers, how-ever, lived in the larger cities, such as Newark, Paterson, Trenton, and Camden, often in slums and barely scraping by. Labor struggles would eventually make the situa-tion better, but there would be a big division in the state between rich and poor through-out the twentieth century.

More growth followed World War I (1914–18) and continued throughout the 1920s. The Great Depression of the 1930s hit the state hard, but the demand for goods and supplies during World War II (1939–45) turned things around once more. Highway construction created roads such as the Garden State Parkway and the New Jersey Turnpike, which helped to lead to the devel-opment of more suburban communities. Then, in the 1960s and 1970s, the decay of

STILL THE GARDEN STATE

Despite being the country's most densely populated state, with many inner-city prob-lems to deal with, New Jersey still manages to live up to its original nickname. Though both poultry and dairy farming are declining, the state continues to be a large producer of fruits and vegetables. With some 44,000 acres—mainly in Burlington, Gloucester, Salem, and Cumberland counties—under intense culti-vation for vegetable production, New Jersey ranks among the top ten states in the produc-tion of asparagus, bell peppers, spinach, head lettuce, cucumbers, sweet corn, tomatoes, cranberries, and blueberries.

the inner cities became more apparent. Riots occurred in a number of cities during a turbulent time for the entire country.

About one-sixth of all drugs manufactured in the United States are made in New Jersey, which has been called "the nation's medicine chest."

A HOME FOR THE TRUSTS

After the Civil War, New Jersey passed some new and lenient corporate laws that allowed companies to purchase their corporate contracts in New Jersey but to conduct their business elsewhere. The law attracted large "trusts," corporations that organized to eliminate competition and control entire industries. This led to the passage of antitrust laws in many other states. By 1904, 170 of the nation's 318 largest trusts were chartered in New Jersey. Among these were the seven largest trusts in the nation—American Sugar Refining, Standard Oil, Amalgamated Copper, American Smelting and Refining, Consolidated Tobacco, U.S. Steel, and International Mercantile Marine. Because it was the home to so many of these corporations, New Jersey became known as the "mother of trusts."

The economy improved once more with the adoption of a state lottery in 1969 and the approval of casino gambling for Atlantic City in 1976. Today, this densely populated state is rife with business and industry. It has many beautiful suburban communities, yet continues to wrestle with the problems of poverty and pollution. Tourists still flock to Atlantic City and to the fabled Jersey Shore. There is something for everyone—even enough farms to justify calling it the Garden State.

Other Things to Know About New Jersey

- The first professional baseball game recorded in the United States was played at Hoboken in 1846.
- New Jersey is a state of bridges. The George Washington Bridge connects New Jersey with New York City; the Delaware Memorial Bridge links the state with Delaware; the Benjamin Franklin, Walt Whitman, and Betsy Ross bridges all connect New Jersey with points in Pennsylvania; and three bridges connect the state with Staten Island, a borough of New York City.
- The Garden State Parkway and New Jersey Turnpike are the most heavily used highways in the Northeast.
- Almost 100 battles during the American Revolution were fought in New Jersey.
- Samuel Morse invented the telegraph in New Jersey, while the legendary Thomas Edison invented the electric lightbulb, the phonograph, and hundreds of other things while working in the Garden State.

NATURAL RESOURCES: flowers and shrubs, grain, sod, fruits and vegetables, sand and gravel, stone, bluefish, crabs, clams, lobster, flounder, porgy, and weakfish

MANUFACTURED PRODUCTS: chemicals, electric and electronic equipment, processed food, instruments, machinery, rubber, plastics, printing and publishing, and metal and petroleum products

WILDLIFE: black bear, coyote, white-tailed deer, woodchuck, skunk, raccoon, many types of turtles, snakes, frogs, and toads, and a variety of birds and fish

NEW MEXICO

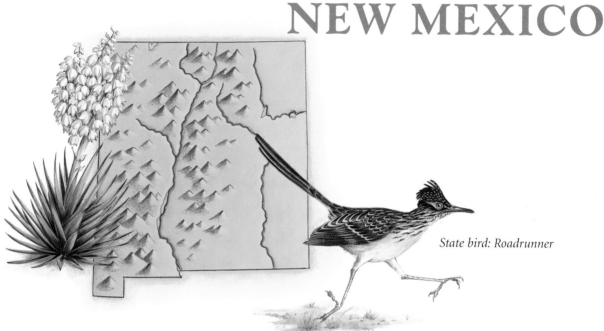

State bird: Roadrunner

New Mexico is a land of plains, plateaus, and mountains, a state in the southwestern United States known for its magnificent and colorful scenery. It is a diverse place, with a population that is composed of Native Americans, those of Spanish descent, and Anglo Americans. There is a multicultural society in New Mexico with many reminders of the past, including the remnants of Native American adobe villages and Spanish architecture. The population of less than 2 million people (thirty-seventh among all the states) is not evenly distributed throughout this fifth largest state. The majority of people live along the Rio Grande, a river that runs toward the Gulf of Mexico and almost through the center of the state, with 39 percent of the population living in the metropolitan Albuquerque area.

Of the lower forty-eight states, only Arizona was admitted to the Union after New Mexico, which became the forty-seventh state on January 6, 1912. Even though the territory was first explored in the sixteenth century—long before the first English settlement at Jamestown, Virginia, in 1607—it took almost another 400 years before New Mexico officially became part of the United States. Today, this nearly square state sits among Arizona to the west, Colorado to the north, Mexico to the south, Texas to the south and east, and a small piece of Oklahoma, also to the east.

When the Spanish first began to explore the Southwest, solely Native Americans lived in the area. There were small expeditions as early as 1528, but the first major one was led by Francisco Vasquez de Coronado in 1540. Coronado found many pueblo communities of Zuni people, but rumors of great riches proved unfounded. Finally, in 1598, Juan de Oñate set out from Mexico (then called New Spain) and took possession of New Mexico for Spain.

By 1610, the capital of the colony was Santa Fe. Relations between the Native Americans and the Spanish were good. They exchanged their wares, and settlers often went into Mexico to exchange goods for European products imported through Mexico City. By the end of the eighteenth century, there was a Spanish population of about 20,000 in New Mexico. Then things began to change.

In 1821, Mexico won its independence

from Spain, leading to the opening of trade between the New Mexico territory and the United States. American merchants began coming to New Mexico via the Santa Fe trail. Trade increased during the 1830s and 1840s, but so did tension between the New Mexicans of Spanish descent and the U.S. citizens. Continued tensions led to war with Mexico in 1846, and when it ended two years later, New Mexico was formally ceded to the United States. It was now a territory under the federal government.

Gold and silver strikes after the Civil War (1861–65) made mining a new and profitable industry. Sheep raising had been the heart of the livestock industry for years, until Texas longhorn cattle were introduced in 1866. After that, large ranches began appearing in the territory. The railroad finally arrived in 1879, bringing even more settlers to the territory. Large-scale irrigation helped both the ranchers and the farmers.

Statehood was a different matter. For years, opponents said New Mexico was a lawless land full of uneducated settlers and dangerous Native Americans. But finally, in 1910, President William Howard Taft supported statehood, and on January 6, 1912, after a long wait, New Mexico became the forty-seventh state. Five weeks later, Arizona became the nation's forty-eighth state. New Mexicans showed their patriotism quickly, with some 17,000 serving in the military during World War I (1914–18). There were about 65,000 New Mexicans in uniform during World War II (1939–45).

During World War II, the state received an economic boost because of federal military installations and nuclear research. In 1943, the government built the town of Los Alamos as a nuclear research laboratory, high in the Jemez Mountains. The first atomic bomb was developed there and tested on July 16, 1945, at Trinity Site in the White Sands Proving Grounds near Alamogordo.

Between 1940 and 1960, the population of New Mexico nearly doubled, and growth continued through the end of the century. By

THE LINCOLN COUNTY WAR

The Lincoln County War might have been just a local feud, had it not included some real-life characters who eventually became legends. It began in 1878, when a sheriff's posse and a gunman hired by a rival rancher and merchant murdered a man named John Tunstall, who had opened a competing store and bank. Tunstall, however, had a group of young bodyguards, one of whom was William Bonny, better known as Billy the Kid. The bodyguards sought revenge and were declared outlaws. Sheriff Pat Garrett captured Billy the Kid in late 1880. He was sentenced to hang, but escaped jail in April 1881, killing two deputies in the process. Shortly afterward, Garrett tracked Billy down and fatally shot him in Fort Sumner, New Mexico. Scores of stories, movies, and television shows have been produced about Billy the Kid, most of them straying far from the real facts.

THREE RIVERS PETROGLYPH NATIONAL RECREATION SITE

The Jornada Mogollon people created these petroglyphs about 1,000 years ago.

the 1990s, political power was concentrated around the state's only metropolitan area, Albuquerque–Rio Rancho. Albuquerque is by far the largest city, approaching 425,000 residents at the turn of the century. Santa Fe, the capital, has fewer than 70,000 people.

The mission church of San Geronimo, one of the earliest in New Mexico, was built near Taos Pueblo in the early seventeenth century.

PANCHO VILLA

In 1916, after New Mexico had become a state, a Mexican rebel named Francisco "Pancho" Villa was embroiled in a power struggle in his own country. When the United States voiced support for Villa's rival, the Mexican rebel led a band of followers over the border and attacked the town of Columbus. Prior to that he had executed sixteen U.S. citizens. President Woodrow Wilson then sent an expedition of federal troops under General John J. Pershing to pursue Villa into Mexico. But because Villa was still a hero to many Mexicans, and because the Mexican government did not like Pershing's presence on Mexican soil, Villa was never caught. He was later pardoned by a new Mexican government and was given a ranch in 1920 as part of an agreement that he retire from politics.

New Mexico is still one of the poorest states in the country, with funding for health and education especially lacking. The traditional sources of revenue—agriculture, ranching, mining, and timbering—are slowly being replaced by high-tech manufacturing and tourism. Native Americans in New Mexico are also working hard to improve their economic situation. They have bought shopping centers, built resorts and gambling casinos, and have invested in real estate. The land, however, is still beautiful.

Other Things to Know About New Mexico

- The deepest cave in the United States is located at the Carlsbad Caverns in southeastern New Mexico. The caverns also have the largest and most extensive underground caves and corridors in North America.
- Santa Fe is the oldest capital city in the United States.
- Almost one-fifth of New Mexico's land consists of forests, with Ponderosa pine the most prevalent wood for processing.
- Rumors of a manned alien spacecraft crashing near an army base at Roswell in 1947 just won't die. Though the army insists it was just a weather balloon that crashed, the incident has been the subject of numerous books, movies, and even a television series in recent years.
- A bear cub rescued in May 1950, from a forest fire in the Lincoln National Forest, was the inspiration for Smokey Bear, the living and later animated symbol of fire prevention.

NATURAL RESOURCES: beef cattle, grain, hay, cotton, lettuce, apples, milk, peanuts, pecans, peppers, potatoes, copper, natural gas, petroleum, potash, sand and gravel, and uranium

MANUFACTURED PRODUCTS: processed food, electric and electronic equipment, and lumber and wood products

WILDLIFE: black bear, mountain lion, mule deer, white-tailed deer, pronghorn, antelope, elk, fox, coatimundi, bobcat, cougar, bighorn sheep, blue grouse, flammulated owl, northern pigmy owl, wild turkey, bald eagle, a variety of hawks and falcons and many small birds, and a variety of trout and kokanee salmon

NEW YORK

State bird: Bluebird

Rich in a history going back hundreds of years, New York has always played a major role in the growth and development of the United States. Though sections of the northern and westerns parts of the state are still sparsely populated and retain a rural character, New York City is the largest city in the nation, with close to 7.5 million inhabitants. And while New York is just the twenty-seventh largest state in size, it is the third most populated (behind California and Texas); more than 18 million people call themselves residents of the Empire State.

New York City is one of the world's leading commercial, cultural, and financial centers, with a host of activities in its five boroughs. It is also the home of the United Nations, the New York Stock Exchange, scores of theaters, the Lincoln Center for the Performing Arts, the Empire State Building, a number of internationally acclaimed museums, and a host of professional sports teams. In addition, there are five other cities in New York State with populations of more than 100,000 each, including the state capital of Albany.

Though New York is considered to be situated in the Middle Atlantic region, the northern part of the state touches the Canadian border. In fact, the Empire State touches a little bit of everything—an ocean, two great lakes, another country, and five other states. The Frenchman Samuel de Champlain was the first to explore the northern boundaries of present-day New

York in 1603. In 1609, he discovered what is now called Lake Champlain. That same year, Englishman Henry Hudson sailed up the river that now bears his name, probably going as far as Albany.

It was the Dutch West India Company that, after hearing Hudson's reports, first sent colonists to the New York area in 1624. They settled at Fort Orange, near present-day Albany. A year later, another group of Dutch colonists settled on the lower tip of Manhattan. In 1626, the governor of the New Netherland colony, Peter Minuit, purchased the island of Manhattan from the Native Americans who lived there for the grand sum of $24. In 1664, King Charles II of England looked at some of the surrounding English settlements and decided he wanted the entire region. He sent four ships and 400 soldiers into New York Harbor. The Dutch citizens didn't resist, and the settlement known as

New Netherland was renamed New York, after the English Duke of York.

New York continued to play a major role in the development of the new land. Many battles in the French and Indian War (1754–63) were fought in New York, as were major battles in the American Revolution (1775–83). On July 26, 1788, New York became the eleventh state to ratify the Constitution of the United States. The state continued to grow rapidly. From 1820 to 1860, New York was deluged by immigrants from Europe, making New York City the nation's largest city with a population of one million by 1860. Nearly half the residents were foreign born. By that time, the entire state had more than 3.8 million inhabitants. New York had already emerged as the primary center of the nation for textile manufacturing and ready-made clothing, banking, insurance, imports, and the stock exchange.

New York also contributed mightily to the Union effort in the Civil War (1861–65). After the war, the growth of the state, especially New York City, continued. Millions more immigrants came. After 1886, those coming into New York Harbor saw the magnificent Statue of Liberty standing on its own island, a gift to the United States from France. By 1910, the population of New York City was an amazing 5 million people. Though there was great wealth and industry, members of the working class often had a difficult time making ends meet, and in the early twentieth century, there was a huge struggle between labor and management. Many African Americans also migrated to the city from the South, and the neighborhood of Harlem soon became a center for black cultural life, with writers, artists, and musicians all finding a place to work and contribute to American culture.

New York also dominated American politics at a crucial time. Franklin Delano Roosevelt was elected governor in 1928. Four years later, he became president of the United States, then was re-elected three times. He died in office in 1945, shortly before the end of World War II (1939–45).

Today the state continues to play a huge role in American life. But much about New York changed on September 11, 2001, when terrorists hijacked two commercial jet liners and piloted them into both towers of the World Trade Center in New York City's financial district. The buildings collapsed, causing the deaths of some 3,000 people and temporarily crippling the city's economy. New York City, however, is showing its resilience by bouncing back with a strong

HEROISM IN THE WAKE OF TRAGEDY

When two airliners hijacked by terrorists crashed into both towers of the World Trade Center on September 11, 2001, the rest of the country saw a side of New York City they had never seen before. Though about 3,000 people died in the tragedy, reports of new heroes emerged daily. Several hundred city firefighters and police officers lost their lives when they responded to the initial call and were caught in the towers' collapse. Others raced to the scene to help and were never heard from again. Firefighters and other volunteers searched the debris for survivors. People came from all parts of the country to help New Yorkers in the wake of tragedy. Patriotic fervor swept the nation. Professional athletes and entertainment celebrities visited the scene and comforted families that had lost loved ones. There were heroes from all walks of life with a common goal—to help in a time of need.

NATIVE AMERICANS UNITED

Like many other states, New York had a fairly large Native American population before the first Europeans came. But in the New York region, something rather unusual happened more than 400 years ago. In about 1570, five of the groups—the Mohawk, Oneida, Onondaga, Cayuga, and Seneca—united to form the Iroquois Confederacy, which was also known as the Five Nations. Located in central New York, the Five Nations began to extend their domain during the seventeenth century, conquering nearly all other Native American groups in the vast area that extended from the Atlantic Ocean to the Mississippi River and from the Saint Lawrence River to the Tennessee River. At some point during the early eighteenth century, the Tuscarora joined the alliance, which then became the Six Nations. The Six Nations remained a force right through the American Revolution. The French and Indian War, then the American Revolution, caused a split in the Confederacy. After the Revolution, those Iroquois who sided with the British fled to Canada, and those who remained were confined to reservations.

Niagara Falls, located on the New York–Canadian border, is one of the natural wonders of the world, drawing millions of visitors each year.

sense of community and courage, and a vow not to let terrorists affect a way of life that has been growing and developing for centuries.

Other Things to Know About New York

- The first pizza restaurant in the United States opened in New York City in 1895.
- Despite being the third most populated state, New York has not abandoned farming; it ranks among the top ten states in production of potatoes, grapes, and apples.
- New York City has the world's most extensive subway system.
- New York has the most extensive library facilities in the United States, including the New York Public Library in New York City, which is the largest public library in the nation.
- The National Baseball Hall of Fame and Museum is located in Cooperstown, New York.
- Ellis Island, in New York Harbor, was long the arrival point for immigrants coming to the United States. Between 1892 and 1954, some 20 million people stepped onto American soil there. In 1990, it reopened as a museum.
- Four U.S. presidents were born in New York State—Martin Van Buren, Millard Fillmore, Theodore Roosevelt, and Franklin Delano Roosevelt.

NATURAL RESOURCES: beef cattle, corn, eggs, milk, flowers and plants, poultry, fruits and vegetables, maple syrup, bluefish, clams, crabs, flounder, lobster, clay, salt, sand and gravel, stone, zinc, garnets, and talc

MANUFACTURED PRODUCTS: chemicals, clothing, electric and electronic equipment, processed food, instruments, machinery, metals, photographic equipment, printing and publishing, transportation equipment, jewelry, and metal, paper, stone, clay, and glass products

WILDLIFE: black bear, white-tailed deer, coyote, bobcat, river otter, muskrat, whale, dolphin, seal, bald eagle, peregrine falcon, and a variety of fish, birds, and reptiles

NORTH CAROLINA

State flower: Dogwood

State bird: Cardinal

Located on the eastern seaboard, in the southeastern portion of the United States, North Carolina was one of the original thirteen colonies and the twelfth state to join the Union following the American Revolution (1775–83). North Carolina is bounded by Virginia, Tennessee, South Carolina, and Georgia, so it is not surprising that it has a southern tradition dating back to the country's beginnings. The state also has a picturesque 301-mile coastline on the Atlantic Ocean and a tidal coastline including islands, bays, and river mouths that stretches for 3,375 miles.

From colonial times right into the 1920s, agriculture was the dominant force in the state's economy. It was only in the late 1920s that manufacturing began to surpass farming as a source of income. By the 1950s, manufacturing was a primary source of jobs as well. Late in the twentieth century, government, commercial and financial services, and tourism also became important economic activities as the state continued to diversify. Today, North Carolina is the second largest industrial state in the South (behind Texas), and is one of the primary manufacturing states in the nation.

Explorers sailed the North Carolina coastline as early as 1524, noticing even then that the land might be good for colonization. In 1585, Sir Walter Raleigh led a group of 108 Englishmen to Roanoke Island. It was the first attempt to colonize North America. But life on the island proved to be too tough, and all but eighteen men returned to England. A second colony arrived in July 1587, but was again unsuccessful. Then, in 1629, King Charles I of England partitioned a section of Virginia south of Albemarie Sound and named it *Carolana,* after himself. The area remained unsettled, however, until the 1650s when settlers came down from Virginia.

By 1729, there were some 35,000 settlers in the area. They quickly established towns, and North Carolina took its place as one of the thirteen original British colonies in America. By the 1760s, however, settlers in the area were tiring of British taxation—as were people in the other colonies. The unrest led to the signing of the Declaration of Independence on July 4, 1776, and the beginning of the American Revolution.

During the war, North Carolinians helped repel two invasions by the British. When the war ended, it became the twelfth state to ratify the Constitution and enter the Union. It was the fourth most populated state in the new nation.

During the early 1800s, North Carolina showed a tendency to favor states' rights over a strong federal government. Toward the middle of the nineteenth century, it was one of the southern states that strongly supported the right to keep slaves. Shortly after the outbreak of the Civil War (1861–65) in April 1861, the state seceded from the Union and joined the Confederacy. During the war, North Carolina lost 40,275 men—roughly one-fourth of all Confederate casualties—though few battles were fought on its soil.

After the war—as sharecropping and tenant farming replaced the old plantation system—the state struggled economically. This new system of farming would stay in place until World War II (1939–45), when farms were finally mechanized on a widespread basis.

The change from an agricultural to a manufacturing economy in the late nineteenth century was a necessary move, and by the 1920s, the state as a whole was profiting. It became a national leader in the manufacture of textiles, tobacco products, and furniture. The Great Depression of the 1930s greatly slowed the state's economy until World War II revived the economy (as it did in many places), with the

THE MYSTERY OF THE LOST COLONY

When Sir Walter Raleigh asked Queen Elizabeth I for permission to choose a site for a colony in 1584, he thought he had found the perfect spot at Roanoke Island. But the first colony of 108 men who landed in August 1585 found it difficult to live there and returned to England, leaving just eighteen men behind. In July 1587, a second group of more than 100 settlers, led by John White, arrived. About two months later, White sailed for England to get more supplies. He wouldn't return for three long years. When he returned in 1590, the entire colony had disappeared. The only clue was the single word *Croatoan,* carved on a tree. Some felt the colonists had gone to live with the Croatoan, a friendly group of Native Americans who lived on nearby Croatan island. Yet a later expedition to the Island showed no trace of the colonists, who, to this day, are remembered as the Lost Colony.

federal government spending almost $2 billion in North Carolina for war supplies.

The 1950s and 1960s were marked by the Civil Rights movement throughout the South. The University of North Carolina admitted African Americans for the first time in 1955. One of the movement's most successful techniques—the mass sit-in—was first introduced in Greensboro in 1960. It

A pier at Nags Head, on the Outer Banks

would take years, however, for many of the vestiges of segregation to fall away, making the battle to end segregation in North Carolina similar to that in other southern states.

By century's end, North Carolina's rate of population increase was one of the highest in

The Old Well stands at the heart of the University of North Carolina campus at Chapel Hill.

THE SHOT

The championship game of the 1981–82 NCAA college basketball season was played between Georgetown University and the University of North Carolina. While there were several stars on both teams, the outcome would be determined by the skills of a North Carolina freshman forward named Michael Jordan. It was a close, hard-fought game from the opening tap that finally came down to the last shot. With just thirty-two seconds left and Georgetown leading by one point, 62–61, North Carolina had perhaps its final chance. As time ticked away, the ball wound up in the hands of freshman Jordan, who took a jump shot from fifteen feet out with just seventeen seconds left. Swish! The clutch basket gave North Carolina the National Championship and helped send Jordan on to a fabled professional career with the Chicago Bulls, where he retired with six championship rings and the label as the greatest player of all time. Yet in the state of North Carolina, Michael Jordan is most remembered for that last-second jumper he took as a freshman, still referred to even today as, simply, The Shot.

the land—and it was already the eleventh most populated state in the nation. The state continues to be among the leaders in production of tobacco, textiles, and furniture. The economy, however, has diversified as the professional and high-tech job sectors continue to grow. Nevertheless, North Carolina continues to have a large rural population, with an infant mortality rate higher than the national average. It also has one of the nation's largest percentages of trailers, or mobile homes, used as housing units. There is still work to be done to secure a more uniform economy.

The state continues to be mixture of old and new. The place where pirates once hid among the sandbars and shoals is the same place where an African American freshman named Michael Jordan made a last-second basket, to give the University of North Carolina a national basketball championship.

Other Things to Know About North Carolina

- The first successful airplane flight was made in 1903 near Kitty Hawk, by Orville and Wilbur Wright.
- Just offshore from Cape Hatteras are the treacherous Diamond Shoals, the site of many shipwrecks through the years. It has earned the nickname The Graveyard of the Atlantic.
- The world's largest furniture market, at High Point, attracts buyers year round from all over the United States.
- Present-day North Carolina has some 70,000 Native Americans, who have organized into nine or more governments or corporations.

NATURAL RESOURCES: tobacco, wood, corn, eggs, milk, turkeys, hogs, chickens, soybeans, peanuts, clams, crabs, flounder, shrimp, clay, gemstones, feldspar, mica, phosphate, sand, gravel, and stone

MANUFACTURED PRODUCTS: chemicals, electric and electronic equipment, processed food, furniture, machinery, medicines, rubber, plastics, textiles, and tobacco products

WILDLIFE: deer, bear, wild boar, alligator, rattlesnake, water moccasin, wild turkey, and a variety of birds and fish

NORTH DAKOTA

State bird: Western meadowlark

Located in the western north central part of the United States, North Dakota is the eighteenth largest state in the Union, but ranks forty-seventh in population. People from other parts of the country listening to weather reports often hear that the city of Bismarck, located in the south central part of the state, has the coldest temperature in the entire country. Winters can indeed be cold, but North Dakota also has some of the best farmland in the nation. It is the second largest producer of wheat, and has always depended heavily upon agriculture for the bulk of its economy.

One of the last states to be settled, North Dakota had a population of only 2,500 white settlers as late as 1870. The history of the state lags behind that of many others, with most of its important developments occurring during the twentieth century. Because North Dakota is so sparsely populated and is located far from large consumer centers, there has been little growth in manufacturing (the state ranks forty-seventh in that area). In fact, most industries in the state are tied directly to agriculture.

Perhaps the most valuable natural resource in North Dakota is its deep, dark, rich soil. Developing naturally under prairie grasses for many years, the soil is among the best in the world and makes it possible to produce abundant crops. This rich soil is especially prevalent in the eastern part of the state.

The first Europeans to enter North Dakota were French explorers in 1738, but after that no others came to the area for more than fifty years. After the United States took over the territory (following the Louisiana Purchase from France in 1803), the Lewis and Clark Expedition entered the territory. The famous explorers spent the winter of 1804 and 1805 living in villages of the Mandan and Hidatsa people.

The first settlers were fur traders. They built a succession of trading posts throughout the area up until the late 1830s, when the fur business began to decline. Until the 1840s, white settlement was limited mostly to areas along the Missouri River. More settlers began coming in the late 1840s and 1850s. Finally, on March 2, 1861, President James Buchanan signed an act that established the Dakota Territory. It included all of present-day North and South Dakota, as well as large portions of Wyoming and Montana. In 1868, the Wyoming Territory was created, establishing the western boundary of the

The top three sunflower-producing states are North Dakota, South Dakota, and Kansas.

Dakotas. The southern boundary wasn't fixed until 1882.

There was, however, no rapid growth in population. The combination of the Civil War (1861–65) and a series of wars with Native American groups helped keep other people from coming to the area. A small group of farmers had set up a community at Pembina in 1851, but as late as 1870, the colony numbered just 2,500 settlers and farmers. It was only after the arrival of the railroads in the 1870s and 1880s that rapid agricultural development began in the eastern part of North Dakota. Wealthy businessmen began creating huge farms that encompassed thousands of acres. These bonanza farms, as they were called, needed hundreds of workers to plant and harvest wheat, and they were very profitable.

These jobs attracted workers from the eastern United States, as well as immigrants from Europe (especially from Norway), and later, ethnic Germans from Russia, Czechs, Ukrainians, and others. In 1900, the population had increased to 320,000 and over the next ten years to 570,000. By that time, both North and South Dakota had become the thirty-ninth and fortieth states, joining the Union on November 2, 1889. North Dakota continued to grow as primarily a farming state.

During this same period—especially once the railroad came in—the cattle-raising industry began expanding. At first there were very large ranches, and business thrived. A major drought in 1886, however, caused a decline in prices. After that, ranches became much smaller. Cowboys disappeared, and beef cattle replaced roaming range cattle.

There was a big demand for wheat during World War I (1914–18), but while most of the country prospered during the 1920s, low crop prices and rising costs hurt the farmers. Then came the disaster of the 1930s, with economic depression, drought, dust storms, and several infestations of grasshoppers. Thousands of small farms

THE RED RIVER ROARS

As with most of the states in the central part of the country, life is often built around rivers, such as the Missouri and Mississippi. Every now and then these rivers show their muscle and create devastating floods. In April 1997, the Red River, which forms the North Dakota–Minnesota border and empties into Lake Winnipeg in Canada, crested at more than fifty-four feet, bringing it some twenty-six feet above flood level. The resulting flood wreaked widespread havoc on many areas, including the cities of Fargo and Grand Forks. Nearly everyone in Grand Forks was evacuated, and the flood caused electrical fires in the downtown section of the city, which destroyed eleven buildings. The flood was so severe that President Bill Clinton made a visit to the area and immediately declared a state of emergency.

went under, and, in some cases, entire towns disappeared.

World War II (1939–45) saw the economy recover somewhat, but beginning in the 1980s, the state has tried to diversify. Food processing has helped the agricultural economy, and, at the same time, energy industries were started for the first time. North Dakota now produces crude oil and has several coal-fired electrical generating plants that sell electricity to neighboring states. In addition, North Dakota has the only significant plant in the country that converts coal to natural gas.

There is still a substantial Native American population in the state, with some 25,000 residents in 1990. Unlike the case in some other states, the Native Americans in North Dakota remain an integral part of the state's society, with some fifty-eight Native Americans holding public offices in 1992.

The International Peace Garden straddles the U.S.-Canadian border of North Dakota and Manitoba.

THE DAKOTA FARMERS' ALLIANCE

Depending on a single industry for an entire state's economy is not always easy, and in North Dakota, farming and agriculture always held the key to the state's fortunes. In the late 1870s and early 1880s, farmers began to feel that the railroads were charging excessive rates to ship goods out of state. (The railroads also owned many of the grain elevators that graded the farmers' grain and set the price.) They also felt that large wheat buyers conspired with the railroads to keep the price low. In 1885, the farmers banded together to found the Dakota Farmers' Alliance. The Alliance was set up to advance the social, educational, financial, and political interests of the farmers. It collected money from farmers to buy coal, twine, and other products as a cooperative venture, and also created its own insurance company to save farmers money on insurance. Working together didn't eliminate the bad times, but the Alliance helped make the farmers' lives better on the whole.

Other Things to Know About North Dakota

- The biggest city is Fargo, with just over 80,000 residents. The state capital of Bismarck has just over 50,000 inhabitants.
- More people work on farms in North Dakota than in any other state.
- The population of North Dakota has actually declined over the past seventy years. In 1930, there were 681,000 people living in the state. According to a 1998 count, there were just over 638,000.
- Hundreds of dams have been constructed in North Dakota for flood control, municipal water supply, and irrigation.
- North Dakota's first radio station, WDAY, in Fargo, went on the air in 1922, within two years of the first radio broadcast in the United States.
- There are more wildlife refuges in North Dakota than in any other state, giving visitors the chance to see bison, antelope, and bighorn sheep, as well as hundreds of different species of birds.
- The Knife River Indian Villages National Historic Site, near Stanton, is the location of large Native American villages like those that were encountered during the Lewis and Clark Expedition, in 1804–06.

NATURAL RESOURCES: wheat, barley, flaxseed, hay, sunflowers, potatoes, beans, beef cattle, honey, milk, oats, sugar beets, coal, petroleum, sand and gravel, and natural gas

MANUFACTURED PRODUCTS: processed food, farm equipment, machinery, electronics, and printed materials

WILDLIFE: elk, moose, bison, wild horse, white-tailed deer, mule deer, antelope, bighorn sheep, coyote, fox, mink, muskrat, beaver, weasel, prairie dog, hawk, owl, eagle, wild turkey, pheasant, and a variety of small birds and fish

State flower: Scarlet carnation

OHIO

State bird: Cardinal

Ohio has one of the most interesting histories of all the states. Because of its location, it became a link between the eastern and western United States, and thus attracted settlers from very different parts of the country. In addition, Ohio's early days saw it making its mark as an agricultural state, but again its location, natural resources, and potential power sources made it a perfect state to industrialize. Thus Ohio went from a leading position in farming to a leading position in industry in a relatively short time. When Ohio became the nation's seventeenth state on March 1, 1803, there were only slightly more than 60,000 people living there. That changed quickly. Ohio soon became one of the most populated states in the country. Seven U.S. presidents were born there.

Ohio's location places it close to several diverse traditional cultures. To the north is Michigan and Lake Erie (on the other side of the lake is Canada). Other surrounding states include Pennsylvania, West Virginia, Kentucky, and Indiana. The name *Ohio* comes from an Iroquois name for the Ohio River, and it means "great" or "beautiful river." The nickname of The Buckeye State was taken from the buckeye trees that were in abundance when the first settlers arrived. None of those early settlers could have imagined what Ohio has become today.

The first permanent white settlement was established in Marietta after the American Revolution (1775–83) in 1788, but difficulties with local Native Americans kept settlers from flocking in. By 1802, the population had grown to 60,000, and a year later, Ohio became a state. It wasn't until after the War of 1812 (1812–15), however, that settlers really began to arrive in large numbers. By 1820, the population had topped 580,000, and ten years later, it was closing in on one million. The Erie Canal had been completed in 1825, providing a link between the Great Lakes and the Atlantic seaboard. With that trade route opened, the state continued to grow rapidly and prosper.

By 1850, Ohio led all states in the production of corn, wool, horses, and sheep, and was one of the four leading states in the production of wheat, cattle, oats, potatoes, and hogs. Adding to the growing prosperity was the arrival of the railroad, which, by 1851, connected most of the state's major cities. By midcentury, Ohio was an agricultural bonanza. That, however, was about to change.

With 2.3 million people by 1860, Ohio

The Rutherford B. Hayes Presidential Center is located in Fremont.

had become the third most populated state in the Union. The largest industry at that point was meatpacking. Ohio was firmly on the side of the Union during the Civil War (1861–65), though very few battles were fought on its soil. In the decades following the war, the state changed its focus, as heavy industry quickly took hold. Northern Ohio became a major center for producing iron, steel, and related products, such as machinery, tools, and metal items.

When John D. Rockefeller founded the Standard Oil Company of Ohio in 1870, the same area became the center of a growing oil refining industry. Other industries that developed in the state were glassmaking in Toledo, and rubber manufacturing in Akron. By 1900, many European immigrants were arriving, looking for work and a better way of life.

It was the growth of heavy industry in Ohio that fostered a strong labor movement. There were now so many workers that they needed organized groups to speak for them. The American Federation of Labor (AFL) was founded in Columbus in 1886. In the ensuing years, labor and industry in Ohio helped the state to dominate national politics. Between 1868 and 1923, seven Ohio

natives were elected to the presidency. Ulysses S. Grant was the first; he was followed by Rutherford B. Hayes, James A. Garfield, Benjamin Harrison, William McKinley, William Howard Taft, and Warren G. Harding.

After World War I (1914–18), Ohio continued to grow and prosper, led again by its strong industrial output. But the Great Depression of the 1930s hit heavy industry

---

OHIO TAKES TO THE AIR . . . AND TO SPACE!

Ohio residents have a long history of looking upward. In 1903, Orville and Wilbur Wright of Dayton invented and flew the first practical airplane, opening up the world of aviation to everyone. During World War I, Eddie Rickenbacker of Columbus became America's leading combat—or "ace"—pilot, shooting down twenty-six enemy aircraft. On February 20, 1962, John H. Glenn of New Concord became the first American to orbit the earth in a spacecraft. Glenn later became an Ohio U.S. senator. Seven years after Glenn's journey, Neil Armstrong, of Wapakoneta, became the first human to set foot on the surface of the moon. From the Wright Brothers to Neil Armstrong, Ohio has helped people go higher and higher in their quest to learn about the unknown.

110

hard, and more than one million Ohio residents lost jobs. Full recovery wouldn't occur until World War II (1939–45), when agricultural production was increased, coal mining rose 82 percent, and industrial employment was up by some 68 percent. After the war, the old industries expanded and new ones developed, including aluminum and chemicals. The opening of the Saint Lawrence Seaway in 1959 gave ocean-going ships a way to reach Ohio's port cities on Lake Erie.

In the 1990s, Ohio was among the top manufacturing states in the nation. New technology also brought about an increase in agriculture, with fewer farms producing greater yields. Turn-of-the-century problems included growing gaps between the rich and poor—a condition felt in many of America's aging cities. But Ohio is a state that has always changed, modernized, and found ways to help its people. If history is any barometer, Ohio will solve its problems and continue to prosper into the twenty-first century.

Industrial and urban wastes substantially polluted Lake Erie by the mid-twentieth century, and the fish population rapidly declined. A concerted effort by the United States and Canada to clean the lake finally began showing results, and recreational fishing and boating resumed in the mid-1990s.

Other Things to Know About Ohio

- Ohio was the home of the first professional baseball team, the Cincinnati Red Stockings, which began playing in 1869.
- The Professional Football Hall of Fame is located in Canton. In the very earliest days of pro football, Canton and Massillon, two small Ohio cities, had the greatest rivalry in the sport.
- While Columbus, the state capital, is officially the largest city in Ohio, the Cleveland metropolitan area (city and surrounding suburbs) is by far the largest populated area, with more than 2.2 million inhabitants.
- The birthplace of inventor Thomas A. Edison and his boyhood home are both preserved for visitors in Milan.

NATURAL RESOURCES: beef cattle, wheat, corn, eggs, hay, hogs, poultry, sheep, wool, soybeans, vegetables, apples, clay and shale, coal, limestone, petroleum, gas, salt, sand and gravel, and stone

MANUFACTURED PRODUCTS: processed food, machinery, metals, electric and electronic equipment, rubber, transportation equipment, soap, machine tools, iron and steel, truck bodies, motorcycles, Swiss cheese, ice cream, and metal, paper, stone, clay, and glass products

WILDLIFE: white-tailed deer, beaver, fox, raccoon, skunk, muskrat, turtle, lizard, copperhead snake, timber rattlesnake, wall-eyed pike, yellow perch, muskellunge, catfish, bass, and large numbers of migrating birds

THE LABOR MOVEMENT IN OHIO

With heavy industry growing so quickly in the second half of the nineteenth century, it was inevitable that the workers would look to improve their lot. Ohio was a leader in the labor movement, beginning with the formation of the American Federation of Labor (AFL) in Columbus in December 1886, during a period of widespread strikes and unrest. The purpose of the AFL was to organize skilled workers into unions; support legislation beneficial to labor; reduce working hours, and improve working conditions and wages. By 1920, the AFL had 4 million members nationwide, and from 1924 to 1952, it was led by William Green, an Ohioan and former mineworker. Other organizations followed the AFL's lead, until almost all industries had representation, political power, and a financial base to support their cause. It all began in Ohio.

State flower: Mistletoe

OKLAHOMA

State bird: Scissor-tailed flycatcher

Perhaps more than that of any other state, the history of Oklahoma is closely linked with the history of Native Americans in the United States. This state in the western area of the south central part of the country was the designated site for many displaced Native Americans during the middle years of the nineteenth century. The name Oklahoma is derived from the Choctaw Indian words for "red" and "people." Oklahoma today has the largest Native American population of any of the lower forty-eight states.

Oklahoma has always been a place of great diversity. Even the land areas vary, from the wooded mountains of the more humid east to the very sparse and dry country of the western plains. Economic activities also differ greatly, from the growing of wheat in the western and central areas, to lumbering, a prime activity in the Ouachita Mountains in the southeastern part of the state. Periodic droughts in the semiarid areas of western Oklahoma, and the dozens of tornadoes that occur on average each year—especially during April and May—create contrasting weather conditions.

All of this adds to Oklahoma's mystique. The capital and largest city, Oklahoma City, has some 470,000 people, while Tulsa has a population of nearly 380,000. They are the only cities with more than 100,000 residents. Yet there wasn't a great influx of white settlers until the final decade of the nineteenth century. In fact, Oklahoma didn't achieve statehood until November 16, 1907, when it was admitted to the Union as the forty-sixth state.

The early exploration of the state followed a pattern similar to that of other states in the area. The Spanish and French held the land first, with the United States taking over the area as part of the Louisiana Purchase in 1803. There was some initial exploration, but no settlement.

Then, after the War of 1812 (1812–15), the U.S. government made the decision to move many Native Americans west of the Mississippi River. They did this to open new lands for white settlers from the East. The original Indian Territory encompassed not only all of present-day Oklahoma, but much of present-day Kansas and Nebraska. After the Civil War (1861–65), the tribes already in Oklahoma were required to open the land to Native Americans being removed from other states and territories.

There soon were problems as the Plains tribes followed the bison and began attacking white settlements. These raids led to more restrictions; chiefs and leaders were exiled to Florida, and the reservation shrank. Finally, in the 1880s, there was a clamor to open the lands of Indian Territory to white settlers. In 1889, Congress opened 2 million acres in central Indian Territory for white settlement. On April 22, 1889, some 50,000 white home seekers raced into the new lands to claim a homestead. Within a generation, Native Americans had become a distinct minority within Indian Territory, and by the 1907 statehood census, the Native American population was only 9 percent of the state.

By the time Oklahoma became a state in 1907, it was the nation's leading producer of petroleum as well as a rich agricultural state. The state continued to grow in population through the 1920s. Then came the drought of the mid-1930s, when plowed fields turned to dust and the wind whipped up huge and debilitating storms, creating what is known as the Dust Bowl. Thousands of farmers and sharecroppers went out of business, leaving the state by the tens of thousands. It would take some forty years for Oklahoma to again

THE FIVE TRIBES

After the War of 1812, the U.S. government decided to move many Native Americans west of the Mississippi River, to open new lands for white settlers. The initial movement involved the Choctaw, Chickasaw, Creek, Seminole, and Cherokee groups. White people referred to them as the Five Civilized Tribes. All five had adopted written constitutions by 1861 and had created communities said to be more orderly than some of the white towns in the West. They developed farms, worked ranches, built towns and schools, and had their own newspapers. Some also kept slaves. During the Civil War, the Five Civilized Tribes supported the Confederacy, and they even sent men to fight. After the war, they were required to end slavery, to allow railroads to cross their lands, and to open their land to other Native Americans being removed from other states. Eventually, however, they too were moved.

reach the population that was recorded in the 1930 census.

Life for other groups has been a battle, as well. African Americans established more than twenty all-black towns during the 1930s, but too often there was violence

The highest concentration of tornadoes is in Oklahoma and Texas.

associated with racial prejudice. By the late 1940s and early 1950s, African Americans had begun to file lawsuits against racial segregation in the public schools. The Oklahoma cases led the way in the eventual landmark Supreme Court decision of 1954, which declared racially segregated schooling unconstitutional.

During the 1970s, the state prospered following a massive grain sale to the former Soviet Union, and in response to the need for crude oil during the 1973 Yom Kippur War between Israel and its oil-producing Arab neighbors. There was another economic dip in the 1980s, when agricultural prices nosedived and oil industry jobs disappeared.

Today, Oklahoma remains more a producer of raw materials than of manufactured goods. Crops and refined minerals are, for the most part, shipped to other states to be made into finished products. Industry, however, is growing slowly but steadily. Aviation, electronics, tire manufacturing, and oil refining are the largest, with only Oklahoma City and Tulsa ranked as important manufacturing centers.

Oklahoma City National Memorial

A TRAGIC ACT OF TERRORISM

On April 19, 1995, Oklahoma City became the site of a devastating and deadly act of terrorism. That morning, without any prior warning, a huge bomb exploded in a truck parked directly outside the Alfred P. Murrah Federal Building. The blast killed 168 people, including many children housed in a day care within the structure, and injured many more. Much of the large building was completely destroyed, creating a very difficult and dangerous rescue mission. A single man, Timothy McVeigh, was convicted of carrying out the terrible bombing because he didn't agree with policies of the U.S. government. McVeigh was executed for the crime in 2001.

Other Things to Know About Oklahoma

- Indian City, near Anadarko, houses the villages of seven different Native American groups. Tourists can observe dances as well as other tribal activities.
- The National Cowboy Hall of Fame and Western Heritage Center is located near Oklahoma City.
- A Cherokee named Sequoya developed a written form for the Cherokee spoken language, identifying sounds and giving each a symbol. Using his methods, the Cherokee became literate between 1821 and 1828.
- There are thirty-five Native American governments in Oklahoma today. They maintain businesses ranging from tax-free tobacco shops to million-dollar bingo operations.
- There are wells pumping oil right on the grounds of the state capitol building in Oklahoma City. The entire city is located on top of oil fields.

NATURAL RESOURCES: beef cattle, wheat, wood, cotton, hay, hogs, milk, peanuts, poultry, sorghum, petroleum, stone, coal, natural gas, gypsum, helium, and iodine

MANUFACTURED PRODUCTS: electric machinery and equipment, processed food, machinery, transportation equipment, petroleum, rubber, and metal, coal, wood, and plastic products

WILDLIFE: pronghorn antelope, white-tailed deer, mule deer, elk, red fox, gray fox, bobcat, beaver, coyote, prairie dog, mink, wild turkey, quail, prairie chicken, pheasant, and a variety of small birds

State flower: Oregon grape

OREGON

State bird: Western meadowlark

A land of uncompromising beauty, with some of the most scenic landscapes in the United States, Oregon also contains fertile soils and rich timberland. In fact, for many years the economy of the area was dominated by its abundance of natural resources.

It was these resources that attracted Europeans to the area in the first place. With the Pacific Ocean to the west, the state of Washington to the north, Idaho to the east, and California and Nevada to the south, Oregon is in the heart of the Pacific Northwest. Though Oregon is the tenth largest state in the country, its population of more than 3.2 million people is mainly concentrated in the fertile Willamette Valley. Some 70 percent of the residents live there, with half the state's population located in the greater Portland metropolitan area, which is located in the middle of the valley.

The Nez Perce were the largest Native American group living in the Oregon area when the first white explorers arrived. They were the first to use horses and travel long distances in search of game; they mounted military campaigns against other Native American groups, including the Paiute and the Shoshone.

One reason that white explorers were drawn to the area was the search for the mythical Northwest Passage—a hoped-for water route that would connect the Atlantic and Pacific Oceans. It was the Lewis and Clark Expedition, which began after the Louisiana Purchase of 1803, that led many Americans to take an interest in the Northwest. The expedition also opened the way to other lands west of the Rocky Mountains. Soon, there were a number of fur-trading posts being set up in the area, which included present-day Oregon. The Hudson's Bay Company became the dominant trading company after 1821, while Fort Vancouver, built on the northern bank of the Columbia River, became the center of a huge trapping and trading business.

By 1842, settlers began crossing the Oregon Trail to the new and fertile land, and within a year, Oregon fever began gripping adventurous pioneers. By the end of 1843, there were some 900 settlers in the area, and more were arriving each year. In 1848, President James Knox Polk signed a bill creating the Oregon Territory, which consisted of the present states of Oregon, Washington, and Idaho, as well as western Montana and part of western Wyoming. By 1850, most of the population of 13,000 was already concentrated in the Willamette Valley. Nine years later, on February 14, 1859, Oregon, with its present-day boundaries, became the thirty-third state of the Union, with Salem as its capital.

Mount Hood

THE BEAUTIFUL MOUNTAINS OF OREGON

The Cascade Range, which extends the entire length of the state, contains some of Oregon's most incredible scenery. The high level of the range is about 5,000 feet, but some sharp volcanic peaks extend even farther toward the sky. Mount Hood, at 11,239 feet, is the highest peak in the state. Mount Jefferson and a series of three peaks called the Three Sisters are all more than 10,000 feet high. Today, there are east-west highways through the mountain passes that provide fairly easy travel except in winter, when the passes can be blocked by snow. The Cascades, along with the Blue Mountains of northeastern Oregon, have a highland climate, with cool summers and very severe winters. Snow is heavy—as much as fifty feet can pile up during the winter. As they have been for thousands of years, the mountains of Oregon are truly breathtaking.

Growth wasn't always easy. There were problems with the Native Americans that lasted until 1877, when the Nez Perce were forced away from their lands and onto a reservation. The economy was beginning to pick up. Gold had been discovered in eastern Oregon in 1860, and the Civil War (1861–65) created the need for manufactured woolen goods, which helped the textile industry in Salem to grow. The coming of the railroads in 1883 readily connected Oregon with other parts of the country. By the end of the nineteenth century, timber was nearly depleted in the Midwest. That was when the logging industry moved into the Northwest. Between 1889 and 1909, timber cut in Oregon increased 4,000 times, with Douglas fir and Ponderosa pine providing the major crop.

Farming and lumbering continued as the main sources of Oregon's economy through World War I (1914–18) and the 1920s. The Great Depression of the 1930s saw President Franklin Delano Roosevelt's New Deal program result in reforestation, soil conservation, irrigation, and flood and forest control for the state. Highways and recreational areas were built, as well as the Bonneville Dam, which created electricity from the power of the Columbia River. This enabled the state to increase industrial production during World War II (1939–45). Portland became a shipbuilding center and the hub of a number of other wartime industries.

Beginning in the 1960s, Oregon's legislature realized it had to begin protecting its wondrous natural resources. Antipollution bills were passed in 1973. The Willamette River Greenway Act was passed to preserve riverbanks from haphazard development. Oregon also became the first state to adopt statewide land-use zoning. Then, in 1975, Oregon became the first state to prohibit the sale of aerosol cans containing fluorocarbons—chemicals suspected of posing a threat to the earth's ozone layer. It was not so

Crater Lake, located at the top of Mount Mazama—an extinct volcano in the Cascade Range—is the deepest lake in the United States with a depth of about 1,932 feet.

long ago that Oregon was a pristine, unspoiled state. Today, its residents want to keep it that way as much as possible.

Another reason for strong conservation measures is that agriculture, forest products, and now tourism are the three main sources of income. New high-tech industries have also come to Oregon because of its inexpensive land and power, its educated workforce, and a very positive business climate. And, as has been true since the mid-1880s, most of this business takes place in the Willamette Valley.

THE BEAVER STATE

Though the origin of the name *Oregon* is uncertain, there is no doubt where the nickname of The Beaver State came from. In the early part of the nineteenth century, trappers or mountain men came into the area and saw the abundance of beaver. Back in the East, everybody wanted fur hats, and beaver were trapped vigorously to supply the growing market. The beaver supply was all but exhausted when the rage for the hats finally passed. But the beaver represents the first example of people using Oregon's natural resources for profit—and a nickname.

Other Things to Know About Oregon

- More than 12 million people visit Oregon each year.
- Barbara Roberts was Oregon's first woman governor, elected to office in 1990.
- Oregon has eleven national wildlife refuge areas that protect mammals and migratory fowl.
- The *Oregon Spectator,* which opened its doors in Oregon City in 1846, was the first newspaper published west of the Rocky Mountains.
- The Wallowa-Whitman National Forest, on the Idaho border in the northeastern part of the state, has one of the deepest gorges (7,900 feet) in the world.

NATURAL RESOURCES: beef cattle, milk, hay, wheat, vegetables, shrubs and seedlings, wood, crabs, rock fish, salmon, shrimp, tuna, pumice, sand and gravel, stone, nickel, and Oregon sunstone

MANUFACTURED PRODUCTS: industrial machinery, electronic equipment, processed food, lumber, and wood and paper products

WILDLIFE: white-tailed deer, mule deer, Rocky Mountain elk, pronghorn antelope, upland game birds, bear, cougar, coyote, beaver, wildcat, migratory birds, pheasant, and quail

PENNSYLVANIA

State bird: Ruffed grouse

As one of the original thirteen colonies, Pennsylvania played a major role in the formation of the United States. A place that was originally settled by people seeking the freedom to worship as they pleased, it was also the place where the Declaration of Independence was written and adopted. There are so many "firsts" in the Commonwealth of Pennsylvania that they are difficult to catalog.

A Middle Atlantic state, Pennsylvania was also located right in the middle of the original thirteen states, with six states to the north and six more to the south. No wonder it was the center of so much early activity. It is surrounded by New York, New Jersey, Ohio, West Virginia, Virginia, Maryland, and Delaware. In the southeastern corner of the state sits Philadelphia, the fifth largest city in the nation as well as one of the most important.

Both French and Dutch explorers traveled into present-day Pennsylvania in about 1615 and 1616, but the official founder of Pennsylvania was Quaker leader William Penn. He was the son of a wealthy English admiral, Sir William Penn. On March 4, 1681, King Charles II signed a charter that made Penn the Proprietor of Pennsylvania, a name given to honor his father, Admiral Penn. Penn called his settlement the "Holy Experiment" and promised religious tolerance for anyone who wanted to settle there. Penn also got along well with the Native

Americans. Because of their help, Penn's colony suffered virtually no periods of hardship and starvation (as was so prevalent in other colonies). It was a good beginning.

After William Penn's death in 1718, there were conflicts among various groups of settlers that lasted through the first half of the century. The French and Indian War began in Pennsylvania in 1754, and a number of battles were fought there. Soon after the war ended in 1763, the rumblings for independence began. In the autumn of 1774, Philadelphia, which was then the largest city in North America, was the site of the First Continental Congress. Delegates gathered to protest British laws. Then on July 4, 1776, the Declaration of Independence was adopted in the Philadelphia State House, which is now called Independence Hall.

A number of bloody battles were fought in the colony before the American Revolution (1775–83) was won, and on December 12, 1787, Pennsylvania became the second state to ratify the U.S.

Constitution. By that time, the state already had a diverse economy. Its fertile farmlands made it the breadbasket of the colonies. Other early industries included milling, mining, printing, and shipbuilding. Philadelphia was also the banking capital of the colonies; it would soon become a manufacturing center producing cotton and silk textiles, iron machinery, and pharmaceutical chemicals.

During the Civil War (1861–65),

Pennsylvania was firmly on the Union side, with more than 350,000 men doing battle for the North. A number of important battles were fought on Pennsylvania soil. After the war ended, industry continued to grow. Pennsylvania had vast resources of coal, iron, and petroleum, plus several avenues of transportation to ship all over. The discovery of oil at Titusville in 1859 not only gave America and the world its first oil well, but led to the creation of another huge industry.

In the second half of the nineteenth century, the battle between labor and management escalated, with much of the trouble starting in Pennsylvania. The first national strike in America occurred in July 1877, with workers striking against the Pennsylvania Railroad. It was the start of decades of strikes and violence that spread around the country.

At the turn of the century, immigrants from Europe poured into the United States, many settling in Pennsylvania. African Americans who had lived in the South also came north, looking for work and a better life. World War I (1914–18) saw Pennsylvania's industries supply a large amount of the nation's war materials. The same happened during World War II (1939–45), but a postwar decline in the coal, steel, and transportation industries, as well as the gradual decline in farming, led the

THE BATTLE OF GETTYSBURG

A huge and decisive battle of the Civil War—Gettysburg—was fought in Pennsylvania from July 1 to July 3, 1863. Confederate general Robert E. Lee led his army of 75,000 troops into Pennsylvania, in what he hoped would be a push into the North that would demoralize the Union. He was met by the Union Army of the Potomac, some 90,000 men strong, led by General George G. Meade. The battle raged for three days. On the final day, Lee sent General George Pickett to lead his 15,000-man brigade in a charge against the center of the Union line. The charge failed, and the battle was lost. Lee's forces retreated and never again invaded the North. It was a costly turning point. The Union had suffered some 23,000 casualties (men killed or wounded), while the Confederacy took 25,000 casualties. Only 5,000 of Pickett's 15,000 men survived his ill-fated maneuver. On November 19, 1863, President Abraham Lincoln traveled to Gettysburg to dedicate a national cemetery at the battlefield. Lincoln spoke a few words that would go down in history as the Gettysburg Address, a short but powerfully eloquent speech.

state's economy to change its focus.

In recent years, food processing, manufacturing, and the service industries have risen to spur the economy. Philadelphia—once the nation's largest city—is now the fifth largest. As with other big cities, it struggles with problems of pollution, of the growing gap between rich and poor, and unemployment. And despite a gradual decline, Pennsylvania still leads the nation in steel production.

Independence Hall

SEEING PENNSYLVANIA'S LONG HISTORY

There is still a great deal of Pennsylvania's long history remaining for visitors and tourists to see each year. Independence Hall, which still stands in Philadelphia, was the place where the Declaration of Independence was adopted on July 4, 1776, and it now houses a small museum. The Liberty Bell, which announced America's independence, stands in a pavilion at a mall adjacent to Independence Hall. There is a history park at Valley Forge, northwest of Philadelphia, where George Washington's army spent a freezing winter during the American Revolution. Gettysburg National Military Park marks the historic Civil War battlefield, while Pittsburgh is the site of two historic forts, Fort Duquesne and Fort Pitt. Hopewell Village near Pottstown is a restored nineteenth-century iron-making village. The Daniel Boone Homestead near Reading preserves the boyhood home of one of America's most famous frontiersmen.

Other Things to Know About Pennsylvania

- The first children's hospital in the United States was built in Philadelphia in 1855.
- The world's largest chocolate and cocoa factory is located in Hershey, Pennsylvania.
- In 1891, Pennsylvania was the leading oil producer in the United States, filling 31 million barrels.
- Philadelphia has a population of nearly 1.5 million residents. The second largest city, Pittsburgh, has just over 350,000 people, while the state capital of Harrisburg has just over 50,000 residents.
- One of the world's first commercial radio stations, KDKA, began broadcasting in Pittsburgh in 1920.
- Benjamin Franklin arrived in Philadelphia from Boston at the age of seventeen in 1723. He would contribute to the Declaration of Independence and the U.S. Constitution, as well as becoming a noted author, scientist, diplomat, and philosopher. He made Philadelphia his home until his death in 1790.
- One of the worst floods in U.S. history occurred in Johnstown on May 31, 1889. A dam broke and sent a huge wall of water cascading through the town, killing more than 2,200 people.

NATURAL RESOURCES: beef cattle, eggs, corn, hay, milk, mushrooms, petroleum, limestone, coal, sand and gravel, stone, and natural gas

MANUFACTURED PRODUCTS: processed food, chemicals, electrical equipment, clothing, machinery, metal products, printed materials, and transportation equipment

WILDLIFE: white-tailed deer, black bear, coyote, red fox, gray fox, ermine, weasel, beaver, raccoon, opossum, muskrat, a variety of songbirds, wild turkey, partridge, ruffed grouse, geese, copperhead and rattlesnake, a variety of fish, and several types of salamanders

Amish harvesting wheat

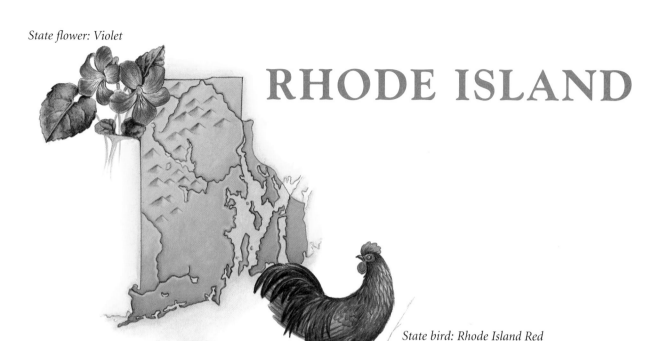

State flower: Violet

RHODE ISLAND

State bird: Rhode Island Red

Rhode Island is not really an island. It is, however, the smallest state in the Union, (with fewer than one million residents), and one of the most highly industrialized. It has a long history, going back to the country's beginning. Located on the eastern seaboard between Massachusetts and Connecticut, Rhode Island's first settlers prospered from the sea—fishing, whaling, and shipbuilding. Yet when the focus of the nation's economy changed years later, the state was able to make the transition to manufacturing and then industry.

The second most densely populated state after New Jersey, Rhode Island is made up of a mainland almost cut in half by Narragansett Bay, and thirty-six small islands—many of which are beautiful and unspoiled. There is also solitude to be found in the many inlets of the bay, the lagoons and salt marshes along the Atlantic Ocean, and the rolling hills of Block Island, a vacation paradise that sits about ten miles out to sea.

Roger Williams, an Englishman, founded the first colony in the area in 1636. Williams originally came to Rhode Island from Massachusetts after fleeing religious persecution. He negotiated with Native American groups—whom he considered his equals—for a large grant of land, and he established the first permanent white settlement at Providence. Williams learned the language of the Native Americans and dealt fairly and

honestly with them. Two years later, another group started a settlement at Portsmouth; a year after that, a group founded Newport; and in 1642, a fourth settlement started at what was then called Pawtuxet (and was later renamed Warwick).

These settlements eventually united and formed their own charter in 1663. Throughout the colonial period, Rhode Island was a place where religious sects who were persecuted in other colonies could live and enjoy the freedom to worship as they chose. There were fewer than 1,000 settlers living in Rhode Island at the time of the 1663 charter. By 1700, the number had increased to about 7,000. There were five new towns by that time, and the population continued to increase. When the American Revolution (1775–83) began, the population had risen to nearly 60,000.

During the early eighteenth century, residents made their living by fishing and farming. They were soon producing surplus livestock and crops, sometimes aided by slave labor. They produced corn, wool, cheese, and horses. In addition, they shipped lumber to the West Indies, England, and southern Europe. With trade flourishing, Newport became a leading social and cultural outlet, as well as a major slave-trading center. That changed slowly during the remainder of the century, and by 1808, when foreign slave trade was banned, most African slaves in Rhode Island had become free.

Rhode Island was the first state to ratify the Declaration of Independence, on July 18, 1776, but was the last of the thirteen states to ratify the new Constitution after the war ended. Many Rhode Islanders opposed a strong federal government in favor of preserving states' rights, and they also opposed the Constitution's original compromises on the slavery question. When they did ratify on May 29, 1790, it was by the narrow margin of thirty-four to thirty-two.

The industrial revolution in Rhode Island began in the late eighteenth century, when Samuel Slater set up the first cotton-spinning plant in the United States. This started Rhode Island on its way to playing a major role in the textile industry. The proliferation of cotton mills brought immigrants seeking work into the state, and the population grew. Other industries that began before the Civil War (1861–65) were cotton printing and dyeing, and the manufacture of woolens, jewelry, and silverware.

During the latter part of the nineteenth century, the economy continued to grow. By 1880, Rhode Island had more workers producing jewelry and silverware than any other state. At the same time, the production of rubber goods began to grow. When the twentieth century began, there were more than 425,000 people in the tiny state, and another 114,000 or so people would move there within the next ten years.

A decline in the cotton industry after World War I (1914–18) signaled the beginning of tough times. Even textile production declined during the 1920s, and the economy as a whole suffered during the Great Depression of the 1930s. The textile decline continued through the 1970s. The closing of the Newport Naval Base and Quonset Point Naval Air Station in 1973 also cost jobs. It was the introduction of high-tech industries in the 1980s that began an economic comeback for the state.

Today, the manufacture of jewelry and silverware remains Rhode Island's leading industry. Many of the country's leading silversmiths work there. Though textile production has declined over the years, the industry still contributes to the state's economy, and a great amount of fine lace produced in the United States is made in Rhode Island. In addition to the advent of high-tech industries, tourism has also become a big business. Rhode Island is now a popular vacation state. Visitors flock to its beaches, historic sites, Block Island, and the resort city of Newport, where some of the opulent mansions from an earlier time now welcome tourists.

Block Island

ONE STATE'S CHANGE OF HEART

As with many of the thirteen original colonies, Rhode Island was using slave labor to help produce crops and livestock in the early eighteenth century. Soon Rhode Islanders were shipping goods to the West Indies in exchange for molasses, which was made into rum at Newport and other places. The rum was then transported to Africa in exchange for black slaves. It wasn't long before Newport became the leading slave-trading center in the colonies. But in 1774, the situation began to change. That year, Rhode Island placed a partial ban on importing additional slaves. Ten years later, a gradual emancipation act was adopted stating that children born to slave mothers after that date would be considered free. Six years later, in 1790, Rhode Island was the last of the thirteen states to ratify the Constitution, because the state's large and influential Quaker population opposed the document's original compromising stance on the slavery question. When Congress finally banned foreign slave trade in 1808, nearly all the blacks in Rhode Island had already achieved their freedom. That was a more than half a century before the start of the Civil War (1861–65).

NATIVE AMERICAN LIFE

When Roger Williams established the first colony of white settlers in Rhode Island, the area was already inhabited by five Algonquian-speaking Native American groups. The Narragansett were the largest and most powerful, with about 5,000 members. Other were the Wampanoag, Nipmuc, Niantic, and Pequot. These groups lived by hunting deer, as well as by catching fish and shellfish. They grew corn, beans, and squash, and moved several times a year between the area's inland and coastal sections. That way, they were able to make use of seasonal resources. Their lives revolved around their village, and each village had a chief, called a *sachem*. It was a structured, orderly lifestyle that became disrupted when more and more white settlers arrived.

The Breakers, a Newport mansion built by Cornelius Vanderbilt II

Other Things to Know About Rhode Island

- The oldest synagogue in the United States, the Touro Synagogue, was founded in Newport in 1763.
- Rhode Island has no large natural lakes.
- Providence is the state capital and largest city, yet it has a population of just over 150,000 people.
- Revolutionary War hero Nathaniel Greene, second in command only to George Washington, was a native Rhode Islander.
- At the Green Animals Topiary Gardens near Portsmouth, there are eighty trees and shrubs cut into the shape of animals.
- The Slater Mill Historic Site at Pawtucket features a restored 1793 yarn mill called the Cradle of American Industry, where visitors can observe hand spinning, weaving, and early textile machines.
- Exactly where Rhode Island got its name remains a mystery to this day. Some feel it may have come from the Dutch phrase *Roodt Eylandt*, which means "red island," because of the red clay on part of the shoreline.

NATURAL RESOURCES: trees and shrubs, sod turf grass, apples, eggs, chickens, potatoes, clams, lobster, flounder, quahogs, sand and gravel, and stone

MANUFACTURED PRODUCTS: jewelry, silverware, electric and electronic equipment, machinery, metal and metal products, and textiles

WILDLIFE: white-tailed deer, moose, black bear, coyote, red fox, mink, opossum, muskrat, skunk, woodchuck, wild turkey, red-tailed hawk, osprey, a variety of sea birds and other small birds, striped bass, blackfish, bluefin tuna, swordfish, crab, lobster, and a variety of smaller saltwater and freshwater fish

SOUTH CAROLINA

State bird: Carolina wren

A southeastern state with a long history, South Carolina would play a large role in the American Revolution, then would spearhead the secessionist movement prior to the Civil War. Always looked upon as a quintessential southern state, South Carolina depended on cotton as its economic staple for many years and remained primarily an agricultural state right into the twentieth century.

South Carolina's climate features hot summers and mild winters. Nearly the entire area was covered with forest through the late seventeenth century, but even today nearly two-thirds of the state's total land area remains forested. Only the fortieth largest state in total area, South Carolina has a population of under 4 million people, with its capital, Columbia, being the only city that tops 100,000 inhabitants.

In 1663, King Charles II granted the land between Virginia and Spanish Florida to eight noblemen, who became lords of the province. The land—originally called *Carolana* in 1629—was called Carolina. The first permanent English settlement began in 1670 at Charles Town (now Charleston). Ten years later, the town was moved from the west bank of the Ashley River to Oyster Point, a better location for defense and trade. By 1700, some 5,000 settlers lived in the area.

In 1729, the Carolinas were separated into two provinces, and during the 1730s, South Carolina grew rapidly. Charles Town was one of the busiest ports in North America, and rice was grown on large plantations with the labor done by African slaves. There were some 30,000 people in the area by 1730. The tidal swamps at the margins of rivers were perfect for growing rice. A second major crop, indigo—used as a source of blue dye—was grown commercially beginning in the 1740s, also utilizing slave labor.

By the eve of the American Revolution (1775–83), South Carolina was a prosperous colony. Support for the Declaration of Independence was mixed until the British attacked Charles Town in June 1776. After that, support for independence grew. During the war, the area was a battleground, and after it ended, South Carolina became the eighth state to ratify the Constitution of the United States, doing so on May 23, 1788.

The invention of the cotton gin in 1793 almost immediately changed South Carolina's economic base, as it did in much

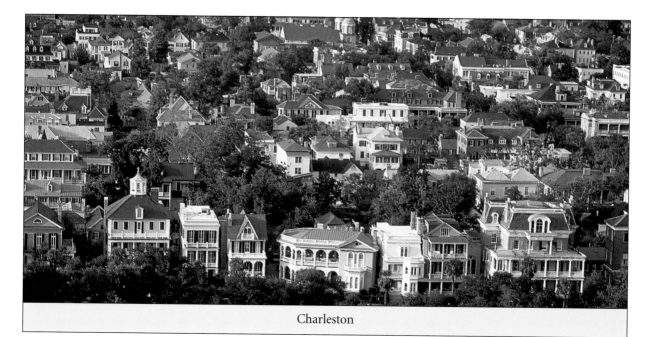

Charleston

of the South. Within a few short years, cotton was planted in almost every part of the state. By 1860, the population was just over 700,000. Sixty percent of the population were African American, and all but about 9,000 were slaves. On December 20, 1860, with the question of slavery dividing the land, South Carolina became the first state to leave the Union. Ten others would follow. The Civil War (1861–65) began on April 12, 1861, when Confederate artillery in Charleston Harbor bombarded federal troops at Fort Sumter.

After that, however, few major battles took place in the state. In February 1865, Union troops under General William T. Sherman burned Columbia during the march northward from Savannah, Georgia. But soon after, the Confederacy was defeated and the war ended. Like other states of the Confederacy, South Carolina was left in deep poverty. It would take the state nearly an entire century to recover.

Though cotton production was resumed after the war, prices were down. Former slaves who had been freed had a difficult time earning a living. Many poor whites became tenant farmers and sharecroppers. They, too, found it tough to make a good liv-

ing. The sharecropping system would last until World War II (1939–45), when agriculture was finally mechanized.

For much of the twentieth century, those who ran the state worked to improve the economy, but at the same time tried to keep strict racial segregation in force. Tobacco became a major crop, but soil erosion wreaked havoc in 1922. The Great Depression of the 1930s only made things worse. Many farmers began migrating to northern cities in search of better jobs.

As with other southern states, South Carolina was a civil rights battleground during the 1950s and 1960s. Slowly, the old ways began to change. Clemson University admitted its first African American student in 1963, and the federal courts ordered total desegregation in the public schools beginning in 1970. Today, South Carolina affords opportunities for all people.

Textiles remain the leading industry, having expanded into the manufacture of synthetic yarns such as Orlon, rayon, fiberglass, and woven plastics. Newer businesses—such as apparel, chemicals, electrical machinery, and fabricated metals—have also helped to change the state's economy. Tourism has become the state's second most important industry, with more than 30 million people visiting the state each year. Yet farming still plays a huge role, with tobacco as the number one crop and cotton still providing raw materials for many manufacturing activities.

The Citadel

PRESERVING THE LAND

As in many states that depend on farming for a large part of their economy, South Carolina often felt the wrath of severe soil erosion. In the past, such erosion ruined large sections of farmland in several strategic areas of the state. In recent years, new ways to preserve and restore eroded farmland have come into use. Now, badly eroded lands are covered with pasture grasses or trees to prevent additional soil from being washed away. Other methods of soil conservation include contour plowing, strip cropping, terracing, crop rotation, and no-till farming. All are designed to keep the soil ripe for producing abundant crops.

NULLIFICATION

In the early decades of the nineteenth century, many individual states still felt that they should ultimately have control of things that affected their economy and way of life. They feared a strong federal government imposing its will. In the decades following the War of 1812 (1812–15), many South Carolinians opposed Congressional tariffs on imports. Since South Carolina exported large amounts of cotton and rice, they feared that high European tariffs in retaliation would hurt their economy. South Carolina native John C. Calhoun, who was vice president under John Quincy Adams in 1828, argued that a state had the right to nullify any federal law that infringed on the constitutional rights of its people. In 1832, after years of opposing tariffs, a state convention declared both of the federal tariff laws enacted in the Tariff Act of 1832 null and void. South Carolina stopped their enforcement in the state, then threatened to secede from the Union if the federal government tried to enforce them. The nullification crisis ended when a compromise bill was passed by Congress in 1833.

Other Things to Know About South Carolina

- More Revolutionary War battles were fought in South Carolina than in any other state.
- Charleston was always a mecca of culture. It had the first museum (1773), and first real theater in America (1736), as well as the first opera (1735) and symphony orchestra (1767).
- Blackbeard and other infamous pirates preyed on ships along the South Carolina coast in the eighteenth century.
- The Andrew Jackson Historical State Park in Lancaster commemorates the birthplace of the nation's seventh president.
- Middleton Gardens in Charleston date from the 1740s and are the oldest formal landscaped gardens in the United States.
- The South Carolina railroad, completed in 1833 and running between Charleston and Hamburg along the Savannah River, was at that time the longest railroad in the world, stretching some 130 miles.

NATURAL RESOURCES: tobacco, cotton, corn, soybeans, fruits and vegetables, beef cattle, chickens, eggs, milk, hogs, wood, clams, crabs, crayfish, oysters, shrimp, snapper, swordfish, wreckfish, clay, sand and gravel, stone, gold, and vermiculite

MANUFACTURED PRODUCTS: textiles, chemicals, furniture, clothing, electrical equipment, rubber, machinery, and metal, plastic, and paper products

WILDLIFE: white-tailed deer, black bear, bobcat, otter, raccoon, skunk, beaver, muskrat, weasel, mink, red fox, gray fox, wild turkey, bobwhite, mourning dove, hawk, owl, bald eagle, Carolina wren, many migratory birds, turtle, lizard, salamander, numerous amphibians, several species of rattlesnake, coral snake, shad, flounder, black sea bass, sea trout, cannel bass, tarpon, sailfish, barracuda, and a variety of freshwater fish

SOUTH DAKOTA

State bird: Ring-necked pheasant

South Dakota did not join the Union until November 2, 1889: until gold was discovered in the Black Hills in 1874, this state in the north central United States had been populated mostly by Native Americans, fur traders, and a handful of settlers. It is a state with two distinct geographical divisions. The Central Lowland, in the eastern half—with a combination of flat and rolling lands, and fertile soil—is very similar to parts of other states in the American Midwest. The western half of the state lies on the Great Plains and includes the Black Hills. Farmland still covers much of the area east of the Missouri River, which divides the state, while vast stretches of rangeland for grazing livestock lie west of the river.

The name *Dakota* comes from a Sioux term that means "friends" or "allies." Modern South Dakota is the fourth least populated state in the Union, and its capital city, Pierre, has a population of just over 13,000. Sioux Falls, with a population approaching 115,000, is the only city that tops the 100,000 mark.

French explorers and fur traders were the first Europeans to enter present-day South Dakota, and that didn't happen until 1742. When they arrived, they found a land inhabited by many Native Americans, most of them part of the Sioux Federation. Sioux people were seminomadic and lived in present-day Minnesota as well as North and South Dakota.

In 1803, the United States took possession of the area via the Louisiana Purchase. The Louis and Clark Expedition traveled up the Missouri River through South Dakota on the way to the Pacific Ocean, and established relationships with the Sioux people. This opened up the fur-trading business. More traders came into the area, as trading posts and forts were built along many of the rivers. In 1861, the Dakota Territory was established. By that time, hundreds of settlers had migrated to the area. New communities sprang up, such as Vermillion, Yankton, and Bon Homme. Many settlers started farming, and Yankton was recognized as the first capital of the territory.

Relations with Native Americans were not always good. Beginning in 1845, the Sioux began to clash regularly with settlers and U.S. soldiers. They didn't want to give up lands they considered theirs. In 1868, the Dakota Territory was reduced to the area of present-day North and South Dakota and a small area was later ceded to Nebraska. The arrival of the railroad brought another wave of immigration of Central Europeans and Scandinavians, beginning in 1873.

A year later, a military expedition led by General George A. Custer discovered gold in the Black Hills. The flood of miners that followed brought more trouble with the Sioux, leading to the Battle of the Little Bighorn in 1876, in which Custer and his men were killed. That battle took place across the border in what is now Montana. Within a year of the Little Big Horn, however, most of the Sioux were defeated. Many of them fled to Canada.

The passage of the Dawes Act of 1887 opened up more land to immigrants. In fact, between 1880 and 1950, the Lakota and Yanktonai groups had to relinquish more than 15.5 million acres of the 21.7 million acres of South Dakota land they had owned. However, as part of the Indian Reorganization Act of 1934, Native Americans in the state were encouraged to organize governments and adopt constitutions. They were also authorized to set up businesses to develop their economy, and a credit program was established to finance tribal and individual enterprises.

More Europeans came between 1900 and 1930, establishing farms and related businesses on former Native American lands. The various groups of immigrants, and those Native Americans remaining on the nine Sioux reservations, made South Dakota one of the most socially diverse states in the West.

The Great Depression and the dust storms that hit the Plains in the 1930s, how-

MOUNT RUSHMORE

Carved into the side of a granite bluff in the Black Hills are the heads of four U.S. presidents. The massive sculpture of George Washington, Thomas Jefferson, Abraham Lincoln, and Theodore Roosevelt sits on the rim of Mount Rushmore in southwestern South Dakota. Each likeness is about sixty feet tall, and the entire memorial cost about $1 million to create. The idea came from South Dakota historian Doane Robinson in the early 1920s. The American sculptor Gutzon Borglum designed the memorial and supervised the construction. Borglum's original design was a sculpture that would depict the four presidents to their waists. The construction was begun in 1927. All the heads except Roosevelt's had been completed when Borglum died in 1941. His son, Lincoln, completed the work that same year.

ever, forced many off their lands. The population of the state dropped by some 30,000 by 1945, to about 590,000 residents. Manufacturing and agriculture were revived during World War II (1939–45), and industrial activity increased as well. New crops and an increase in the raising of cattle and poultry gave a boost to the agricultural industry once again. The state also benefited from the establishment of military bases and other federal agencies. The Army Corps of Engineers built four of six main dams along the Missouri River. This stabilization of the Missouri River created lakes and irrigation, and also helped boost the tourist industry.

Today, South Dakota remains an important agricultural state, but with enough industry and small factories to support the agricultural efforts. Native Americans constitute some 10 percent of the state's population. Various Native American groups have received compensation from the federal government for illegal seizure of lands; they continue to pursue legal channels to right some of the wrongs done to them in the past.

Badlands National Park

Other Things to Know About South Dakota

- The largest working gold mine in the Americas is in Lead, South Dakota.
- A statue of the Sioux chief Crazy Horse is carved on a mountain near Custer.
- Mount Moriah Cemetery, overlooking Deadwood, contains the graves of Wild Bill Hickok and Calamity Jane.
- The world's largest drugstore, Wall Drug in Wall, is internationally famous and a noted tourist stop.
- The state capital, Pierre, is named for Pierre Chouteau, Jr., who became manager for regional trade of the American Fur Company in 1827; he was the most powerful man in the region until his death in 1865.

NATURAL RESOURCES: beef cattle, sheep, hogs, corn, eggs, milk, flaxseed, hay, rye, oats, wheat, soybeans, wool, sunflowers, gold, clay, sand and gravel, and stone

MANUFACTURED PRODUCTS: machinery, electric and electronic equipment, processed food, lumber, printing and publishing, and stone and clay products

WILDLIFE: bison, coyote, elk, white-tailed deer, mountain goat, bighorn sheep, feral burro, bobcat, beaver, antelope, mule deer, fox, prairie dog, Hungarian partridge, Chinese ring-necked pheasant, sage grouse, sharp-tailed grouse, prairie chicken, wild turkey, a variety of small birds, walleye, northern pike, smallmouth black bass, other game fish, and catfish

THE WILD WEST

When gold was discovered in the Black Hills in 1874, a familiar pattern emerged. Within two years, some 15,000 miners had come to the area, all trying to strike it rich. A year later, the white population of the Black Hills reached 25,000. Mining settlements, or boomtowns, sprang up almost overnight. These towns were wild, lawless, and dangerous. It didn't take long before they were attracting all kinds of characters—frontiersmen, marksmen, and lawmen. One was called Deadwood, a name still spoken in western folklore. Two of the most famous western legends who spent time in Deadwood during the gold rush were the lawman Wild Bill Hickok and the sharpshooter and horsewoman Martha Jane Canary, better known as Calamity Jane. The towns died as fast as they were born. Once the surface gold was gone, many of the get-rich-quick miners left—and mining companies began taking the gold from deep in the ground.

State flower: Iris

TENNESSEE

State bird: Mockingbird

Though some two-fifths of Tennessee's population continues to live in rural areas, the nation's sixteenth state is certainly not looked upon as rural. In fact, Tennessee is a diverse and interesting place with a history that has helped shape both the social and cultural fabric of the country. A border state between North and South, situated in the eastern south central region of the country, Tennessee is surrounded by eight other states—Kentucky, Virginia, North Carolina, Georgia, Alabama, Mississippi, Arkansas, and Missouri.

Despite the still large rural population, Tennessee has four major cities—Memphis; the capital, Nashville; Knoxville; and Chattanooga. Three former presidents—Andrew Jackson, James Knox Polk, and Andrew Johnson—lived and are buried in Tennessee. The legendary frontiersman, Davy Crockett, was born there. W. C. Handy, known as the Father of the Blues, lived in Memphis. Legendary rock 'n' roll star Elvis Presley lived and died at his mansion, known as Graceland. The city of Nashville, with the Grand Ole Opry, is the home of America's country music.

English and French explorers began coming to the Tennessee area late in the seventeenth century. There was rivalry for trade with Native Americans, but no real settlement. After the French and Indian War (1754–63), the English took over the region. Oddly enough, the first settlements came despite a ban by the British king on settlement by whites west of the Appalachian Mountains.

First hunters and trappers arrived, followed in 1769 by hundreds of people who built log cabins in the Watauga River valley. Soon more came and negotiated to buy land from the Cherokee. Some came with slaves to work the land, or bought slaves after they settled in. Then, in 1780, while the American Revolution (1775–83) was raging, several hundred settlers established a colony at Fort Nashborough on the Cumberland River, at the site of present-day Nashville.

By 1795, there were some 77,300 inhabitants in the region, including 66,700 who were free. That was more than the 60,000 needed for statehood, and on June 1, 1796, Tennessee was admitted to the Union as the sixteenth state. At the time of statehood, nearly three-fourths of Tennessee lands were claimed by Native Americans. But by 1819, most Native American lands had been ceded to the United States, and the population of the state grew quickly. Between 1830 and 1860, the population increased from 682,000 to more than one million, and the state grew in agricultural importance. It produced corn, cotton, and tobacco, as well as livestock.

The Civil War (1861–65) changed everything. Tennessee wasn't as decisive as some other southern states in wanting to secede from the Union. But after the war began with the attack on Fort Sumter in 1861, Tennessee voted to join the Confederacy. The war would prove very costly for the state. More battles were fought in Tennessee than in all other states with the exception of Virginia. By the end of 1864, Union forces controlled the entire state and remained there until the war ended the following year.

Tennessee was the first Confederate state readmitted to the Union. But, as with other southern states, there were tensions between whites and freed African Americans. The violent, white supremacist vigilante group known as the Ku Klux Klan was organized in Pulaski, Tennessee, in the winter of 1865–66. They would try to block Reconstruction efforts and keep the freed former slaves from obtaining the same rights as whites.

Museum of Appalachia, Tennessee

The state tried to rebuild its agricultural economy through sharecropping and tenant farming. As in other states, this was difficult, but the system would last through World War II (1939–45). There were strikes and continuing economic problems in the late nineteenth and early twentieth centuries. During the Great Depression of the 1930s, the Roosevelt administration created the Tennessee Valley Authority (TVA), an innovative program for regional development. The TVA developed the Tennessee River and its tributaries for navigation, flood control, and the production of electricity.

After World War II ended in 1945, the state began the change from an agrarian economy to an industrial and service one. By 1950, the urban population finally exceeded the rural, and the cities continued to grow. Memphis and Nashville were on the road to becoming major U.S. cities. Still, into the 1990s, nearly half the state's land surface was

SERGEANT YORK

Born in the small town of Pall Mall, Tennessee, in 1887, Alvin York planned to grow up and work the family farm. When the United States became involved in World War I in 1917, many young men rushed to enlist. Alvin York refused, claiming he was a conscientious objector and would not kill for religious reasons. Soon, however, York reconsidered and joined the army. On October 8, 1918, York was in the Argonne Forest in France. Confronted by German soldiers, York and his men captured a machine-gun nest, killing twenty-five enemy solders. Then, acting almost alone, Alvin York captured 132 German soldiers, who were made prisoners of war. The one-time conscientious objector was promoted to sergeant and received more than fifty decorations, including the Congressional Medal of Honor. In 1941, a movie was made about Sergeant York's life and military exploits, and it won an Academy Award for Gary Cooper, who was named best actor for his portrayal of the farm boy turned war hero.

used as farmland, with one-third of that farmland used for crops, which generate one-half of the state's farm income. Livestock and animal products generate the other half.

The production of motor vehicles and parts is now Tennessee's largest industry. Tennessee also ranks among the leading states in the quarrying of marble, and is second behind Alaska in the production of zinc. In addition, the tourism industry has grown, with many historic landmarks—from the

Hikers on the Appalachian Trail

THE SCOPES TRIAL

One of the landmark trials in U.S. history took place in Tennessee in 1925. A year earlier, the state legislature passed a law making it a crime to teach the theory of evolution (that humans evolved slowly from lesser forms of animals) in public schools. A young teacher named John Scopes decided to test the law, and he explained the theory in his class. He was arrested and prosecuted. The ensuing trial received national attention after William Jennings Bryan, a three-time presidential candidate, was named prosecutor; and Clarence Darrow, a renowned defense attorney, was named to defend Scopes. Though Scopes was convicted and fined $100, the conviction was later reversed by the state Supreme Court. The statute against teaching evolution remained on the books until 1967.

Hermitage (the home of Andrew Jackson) to Civil War battle sites to the Grand Ole Opry in Nashville—attracting visitors from around the world.

Other Things to Know About Tennessee

- Frontiersman Davy Crockett was born near Limestone, Tennessee. Tourists can visit not only his birthplace, but three other places in the state where he lived.
- At Cades Cove—a restored village in the Great Smoky Mountains National Park—tourists can see how people lived in pioneer days.
- The Chattanooga *News-Free Press* and *Times* were published in 1878 by Adolph S. Ochs, who later owned and developed *The New York Times.*
- From the top of Lookout Mountain, near Chattanooga, visitors on a clear day can see parts of five surrounding states.
- Dollywood, in Pigeon Forge near the Great Smoky Mountains National Park, is a family entertainment park founded by country-western singer Dolly Parton.
- In 1872, a Nashville barber named Sampson W. Keeble became the first African American to serve in the state legislature.
- In April 1968, civil rights leader Rev. Martin Luther King, Jr., was shot to death on the balcony of a motel in Memphis.
- Tennessee native Al Gore served as vice president under Bill Clinton from 1992 to 2000, and was the Democratic candidate for president in the 2000 election.

NATURAL RESOURCES: cotton, corn, tobacco, hay, beef cattle, chickens, hogs, milk, plants and shrubs, soybeans, zinc, coal, ball clay, and stone

MANUFACTURED PRODUCTS: processed food, machinery, transportation equipment, chemicals, electric and electronic equipment, rubber, printed materials, and metal and plastic products

WILDLIFE: black bear, white-tailed deer, wolf, red fox, mink, long-tailed weasel, muskrat, woodchuck, gray fox, migratory birds, bobwhite, ruffed grouse, mourning dove, turkey; copperhead, cottonmouth, and timber rattlesnake; a variety of turtles, lizards, and nonpoisonous snakes, black bass, carp, catfish, and crappie

State flower: Bluebonnet

TEXAS

State bird: Mockingbird

Texas is big. Very big. In fact, 220 Rhode Islands could fit into the state of Texas. So could Ohio, Indiana, and all the New England and Mid-Atlantic states combined. Until Alaska became a state in 1959, Texas was the largest state in the Union and is still the largest of the lower forty-eight. It is also the second most populated state in the Union, and the only one to have three cities with populations that exceed one million residents.

Many people still think of Texas as a state where cowboys sit tall in the saddle, driving herds of cattle across the plains to market. Yet nothing could be further from the truth. Texas is a thoroughly modern state, industrialized and exciting. It is the home of the Lyndon B. Johnson Space Center and many major corporations. The Dallas–Fort Worth airport is one of the busiest in the world, and there are thirteen deep-water ports along the Gulf Coast.

Located in the western south central United States, Texas borders Mexico on the southwest and the Gulf of Mexico on the southeast. Austin is the capital city, while Houston is the largest city, with a population of nearly 1.8 million. Both Dallas and San Antonio are also over the one-million mark, while El Paso and Austin each have more than 500,000 residents. Big as it is, Texas is still growing.

Spanish explorers were the first Europeans to arrive in Texas, in about 1519. Spain controlled the area until 1821, when Mexico gained its independence and also received rights to Texas. The Mexican government allowed white American settlements, and soon these colonies began to multiply. From 1821 to 1836, the population of Texas increased from about 7,000 to nearly 50,000 inhabitants.

At that time, there was a new dictatorial Mexican leader, Antonio Lopez de Santa Anna. Santa Anna began sending troops to Texas, and he was soon at odds with the American settlers. By November 1835, a group of settlers set up a provisional state government, and the Texas Revolution was under way. After defeats at the Alamo and at Goliad, the Texans under General Sam Houston defeated Santa Anna at the Battle of San Jacinto on April 21, 1836. Santa Anna

REMEMBER THE ALAMO

One of the most legendary battles in North American history was fought during Texas's war for independence against Mexico. On February 23, 1836, a Mexican force of more than 2,000 men reached the outskirts of San Antonio, which had been captured by the Texans the previous December. Badly outnumbered, a Texan force of 155 men withdrew to a former Franciscan mission known as the Alamo. The Mexicans surrounded the mission. On March 1, the Texans were reinforced by another thirty-two men. But the Mexicans began shelling the mission, keeping up the barrage for five days. On March 6, the Mexican army succeeded in breaching the walls. The Texans fought fiercely, but in the end all were killed. Only a few civilians survived. Among the dead were renowned American frontiersmen Davy Crockett and Jim Bowie. Santa Anna lost some 600 men, and a short time later, his army was defeated at the pivotal Battle of San Jacinto. As the Texans rallied to victory, many of them shouted what had become a uniting battle cry: *Remember the Alamo!*

was captured and was forced to recognize the independence of Texas.

For the next ten years, Texas was an independent republic, but it was finally decided that Texas would be better off as part of a larger framework. On December 29, 1845, Texas joined the Union as the twenty-eighth state. It was also officially classified as a slave state. This led to Texas seceding from the Union when the Civil War (1861–65) began. Few battles took place on Texas soil, though the port at Galveston was captured, then recaptured. On March 30, 1870, nearly five years after the war ended, Texas was readmitted to the Union.

In the following years, the population began increasing rapidly. From about 819,000 inhabitants in 1870, the state grew to over 3 million in 1900, making it the sixth most populated state in the country. During

this time, cattle ranching became more important to the economy. The cowboy legend was born when huge herds of cattle had to be driven to market in Kansas over the Chisholm Trail. In addition, the arrival of the railroad made cotton an important crop.

Though Texas was growing and prospering at the outset of the twentieth century, African Americans in the state suffered from increased discrimination, a situation that would continue right into the civil rights struggles of the 1950s and 1960s. As for the economy, it continued to prosper until the Great Depression of the 1930s, when cotton prices dropped and the state had few industries to pick up the slack. Public works projects under the New Deal helped put people back to work. Then came World War II (1939–45), when rapid construction of defense-related factories put the state on the road to industrialization. San Antonio became a center for the U.S. Army Air Force, as more than forty bases were built in the area.

Soon the demand for oil and petrochemicals (chemicals based on oil or natural gas) made the strip from Houston to Lake Charles in southwestern Louisiana the most industrialized area of the South. The need for paper revitalized the East Texas lumber industry, and the need for defense workers helped turn the state away from its rural economic base toward an urban industrialized economy.

Both the economy and population grew rapidly from the mid-1970s through the early 1980s. After a slump in oil caused a business downturn in the mid- to late 1980s, modern-day Texas really began to emerge. High-tech companies, service industries, finance, and trade all began prospering in the 1990s. The cities continued to grow as more businesses came. Then, at the turn of the twenty-first century, a former Texas governor, George W. Bush, became the forty-third president of the United States.

Longhorn steer

Other Things to Know About Texas

- More land is farmed in Texas than any other state.
- It is estimated that almost 10 million bison (American buffalo) were killed in Texas between 1871 and 1880 for sport, food, hides, and to help force Native Americans onto reservations.
- In 1924, Miriam "Ma" Ferguson—wife of former governor "Farmer" Jim Ferguson—became the first woman in the United States to be elected to the office of governor.
- Barbara Jordan of Houston became the first African American woman elected to the state Senate in 1972. She was subsequently elected to the U.S. House of Representatives.
- Because Texas was an independent republic for nearly ten years, it acquired the nickname The Lone Star State, which it still carries today.

NATURAL RESOURCES: beef cattle, cotton, corn, fruit, nuts, hay, greenhouse and nursery products, poultry, sorghum, wheat, rice, crabs, oysters, flounder, red snapper, sea trout, shrimp, natural gas, petroleum, sulfur, and salt

MANUFACTURED PRODUCTS: chemicals, electric and electronic equipment, metals, processed food, transportation equipment, printed materials, and metal, petroleum, coal, stone, clay, and glass products

WILDLIFE: white-tailed deer, coyote, pronghorn antelope, cougar, black bear, prairie dog, nine-banded armadillo, peccary, western diamondback rattlesnake, coral snake, copperhead, cotton-mouth, alligator, turtles and lizards, a variety of small birds, whooping crane, wild turkey, gold eagle, tarpon, shrimp, crab, oyster, catfish, and bass

TEXAS'S CHANGING DEMOGRAPHICS

As in nearly all other states of the Union, the first Texans were Native Americans. Today, however, there is a single, small reservation in the state where a few remaining Native Americans live. Nonetheless, with the second highest population in the land, Texas is becoming more of an international melting pot than ever before. According to experts, it will change even more in upcoming years. By 1990, whites (including white Hispanics) made up 75.2 percent of the population. African Americans made up 11.9 percent, and Asians and Pacific Islanders comprised just 1.9 percent, while those of mixed heritage or not reporting their ethnicity made up 10.6 percent. Hispanics of any race were at 25.5 percent. There has been a continued influx of Hispanic and Asian peoples. Demographers now predict that by the year 2010, the state will have a population made up of 36.7 percent non-Hispanic whites, 9.5 percent African Americans, 45.9 percent Hispanics (of any race), and 7.9 percent of other racial and ethnic groups.

State flower: Sego lily

UTAH

State bird: California gull

Utah was settled by a group of people—the Mormons—who had gone west to escape religious persecution. The Mormons arrived in 1847, and while modern Utah is more ethnically and religiously diverse, Mormons still comprise more than 70 percent of the population. The state is in the western part of the country, situated among Nevada, Idaho, Wyoming, Colorado, and Arizona. With just over 2 million residents, Utah is the thirty-fourth most populated state in the Union. It is also the second driest.

There was very little European or North American activity in the Utah area until the 1820s, when fur trappers began arriving. Soon Canada's Hudson's Bay Company began doing business there. But there was no settlement until the explorer John Charles Frémont, making the first of several trips through present-day Utah in 1843, created maps and collected important scientific data about the region.

The Mormons had originally settled in Ohio, Missouri, and Illinois. They found themselves persecuted for some of their beliefs, and by 1846 they had decided to move west, maybe even to Mexico. In 1847, an advance party of Mormons led by Brigham Young set out to seek an isolated place to settle. Young had read John Frémont's report on the Great Basin. On July 24, 1847, Young and his followers came down from the Wasatch Mountain Range at Emigration Canyon. Before them lay a deso-

late plain. Young looked at the land and announced that it was the right place.

The Mormons established the first permanent white settlement between the Great Salt Lake and the Wasatch Range. Within weeks, more than 1,500 additional settlers arrived and began building what they would call Great Salt Lake City (renamed Salt Lake City in 1868). By 1850, there were more Mormon communities springing up and already some 10,000 settlers. They not only lived in Great Salt Lake City, but also established settlements at Ogden, Bountiful, Provo, and Manti. Ten years later, in 1860, there were some 40,000 Mormons settled in colonies in the Utah region.

The Mormons worked together very closely to build their communities, which were considered communal ventures. Under the leadership of Brigham Young, they created a system of irrigation that would be copied by others. The members also became

Mormon Temple, Salt Lake City

self-sufficient, constructing gristmills, sawmills, tanneries, as well as carding, spinning, and weaving mills. They also built small factories.

In 1849, the Mormons wanted to create a state called Deseret, a name taken from the Book of Mormon. But Congress refused to recognize it. Instead, the Utah Territory was created in 1850, and in 1868 the area was reduced to the size of present-day Utah. However, it would take nearly another thirty years for Utah to officially become a state. The reason: the Mormon policy of polygyny, which allowed a man to have more than one wife. Finally, in 1890, the church leadership issued a decree that advised members to abstain from polygyny. On January 4, 1896, Utah was admitted to the Union as the forty-fifth state.

Between 1900 and 1930, the population of Utah increased from about 277,000 to 508,000. Agriculture was still the leading source of income, but mining and manufacturing had also become viable industries. By that time, many non-Mormons had also

MORMON INGENUITY

In the mid-1800s, many Mormon families arrived in Utah over a very short period of time. They came to a totally undeveloped land and soon had functional communities with productive farms and small factories. Their colonies were all cooperative and communal ventures. They worked to irrigate their farmlands, instituting a system that was so successful, it became the basis for future irrigation laws in the West. Mormon farmers would work together to build central irrigation ditches to draw water off from rivers and mountain streams. Then each individual farmer would dig smaller trenches from the central trough to his own land. Church committees would set the hours for the use of the water by individual farms according to their needs.

come into the state. The Great Depression hit Utah especially hard, with the mining industry affected the most. It took World War II (1939–45) to jump-start the economy once again. Manufacturing and mining were expanded, and several military bases were built. The federal government also built a large steel plant in Geneva, which was sold to private industry after the war and quickly expanded its operations. By 1950, manufacturing had passed agriculture as the main source of income in the state.

Postwar expansion was also due to the defense industry, with the development of guided missiles and other defense installations. The copper-mining industry also expanded, while an oil boom in the 1950s boosted the state's economy. The 1980s saw even more diversity, with the growth of higher education and the arrival of computer industries. The state's natural resources also brought about a marked increase in tourism. Utah took an even greater role in the computer industry in 1995, when the Micron Company announced plans to construct a huge facility at Lehi.

Great Salt Lake

The continued growth of the state at the turn of the twenty-first century has led to increased crime and pollution. Yet despite a very large percentage of school-age children, Utah ranks among the top states in high-school graduation rate and standardized test scores. Preparation for the 2002 Winter Olympic Games at Salt Lake City helped to modernize a strained transportation system and increase facilities for tourists.

Other Things to Know About Utah

- The Great Salt Lake is the fifth largest natural lake in the United States, after the four Great Lakes. It is four times as salty as any ocean, and contains an estimated 6 billion tons of salt.
- A third of Utah is made up of desert, while more than half the land in the state is owned by the U.S. government.
- Rainbow Bridge in Utah is the largest natural arch or rock bridge in the world, standing 290 feet high and spanning 275 feet across the water.
- The Sundance Film Festival, organized by actor Robert Redford, is an internationally recognized celebration of movies held annually at the Sundance Ski Resort and nearby cities.
- During World War II, many Japanese Americans were relocated from the West Coast and held at the Topaz War Relocation Camp in Utah until the war ended.

NATURAL RESOURCES: wheat, hay, turkey, beef cattle, fruit, eggs, hogs, sheep, wool, copper, coal, gold, gilsonite, molybdenite, iron ore, natural gas, petroleum, sand and gravel, and uranium

MANUFACTURED PRODUCTS: petroleum, processed food, electric and electronic equipment, metal, machinery, printing and publishing, transportation equipment, and coal, stone, glass, and clay products

WILDLIFE: mule deer, elk, pronghorn, antelope, moose, bison, black bear, cougar, Rocky Mountain goat, Rocky Mountain bighorn sheep, coyote, bay lynx, Canada lynx, bobcat, gray fox, red fox, kit fox, badger, mink, otter, weasel, prairie dog, sidewinder and western rattlesnake, desert tortoise, collared and horned lizard, Gila monster, migratory birds, California gull, ring-necked pheasant, bald eagle, golden eagle, and a variety of smaller birds

VERMONT

State bird: Hermit thrush

There are only seven states smaller than Vermont, and only one with fewer people. In fact, this New England state, which is tucked between New York, Canada, New Hampshire, and Massachusetts, is small in other ways as well. Its cities are small, its factories are small, and its rural atmosphere has made it a favorite vacation spot for many people in the Northeast. Even with its long history, Vermont has always been a little off the beaten path. It was even a separate country for a period of about ten years before its people decided they wanted to be part of the United States!

Despite the long winters of the Northeast, Vermont was farm country, with agriculture the main economic activity, all the way into the twentieth century. Then industry and manufacturing slowly emerged at the forefront of the economy. Today the service sector—spearheaded by tourism—is the fastest growing segment of Vermont's economy. Yet there are still fewer than 600,000 people in the entire state. The largest city, Burlington, has a population under the 40,000 mark, while the state capital, Montpelier, has roughly 7,900 occupants.

Great Britain established the first permanent settlement in Vermont at Fort Dummer in 1724, on the site of present-day Brattleboro. The colonists were from Massachusetts. The French, who also had claims on the area, subsequently built forts at

Crown Point in 1731 and at Ticonderoga in 1755. In essence, Vermont became a battleground between the French and English as they fought for control of North America between 1689 and 1763. It was the end of the French and Indian War (1754–63) that resulted in the French moving north to Canada and finally opening Vermont for more settlement.

But even after the French were gone, other English colonies competed for control of Vermont. Both New York and New Hampshire made land claims in the Vermont area. That led to more violence, as a local man named Ethan Allen formed a militia force known as the Green Mountain Boys. For five years they fought against land claims from other colonies. The battle ended in 1775, when the American Revolution

(1775–83) began and the Green Mountain Boys turned to fight against the British. Their biggest victory was the capture of Fort Ticonderoga and the fort at Crown Point.

Several more battles were fought in Vermont before the war ended. On January 15, 1777, those living in the area declared their independence from Great Britain and established an independent republic. At first they called it New Connecticut, then they changed the name to Vermont. They also adopted a constitution that became the first in America to prohibit slavery and gave all adult males—not just property owners—the right to vote.

Vermont was akin to a separate country during the entire 1780s, even after the war ended. The original thirteen colonies had formed the United States of America. Finally, on March 4, 1791, after New York gave up all its land claims in the republic, Vermont became the fourteenth state to join the Union.

From 1791 to 1810, the population increased from about 85,000 to 218,000. Most new settlers came from southern New England to start their own farms. Light industry also began developing. Residents produced textiles, iron, lumber, and potash—a wood by-product used for making soap and glass, and for preparing wool. In the years following the War of 1812 (1812–15), many Vermont residents began leaving, especially farmers who had heard about the fertile lands of the Ohio valley.

Irish and French-Canadian immigrants became a source of labor for the railroads and mills, while the lumber business began flourishing in the 1840s and 1850s. Then, after 1865, Italian and Welsh immigrants began arriving to work in the growing industries of marble, granite, and slate quarrying. The state sent about 35,000 troops to fight for the Union in the Civil War (1861–65), though no battles were fought on Vermont

soil. During the last half of the century, lumber and wood production became the state's principal industry.

Vermont grew slowly during the early twentieth century, experiencing the same ups and downs as many other sections of the country. After World War II (1939–45), industry in the state grew steadily, though businesses for the most part remained small. Soon, though, some large industrial companies, such as International Business Machines (IBM), opened new factories in the state. Tourism and the recreation industry also began growing. Stowe and other ski resorts opened in the Green Mountains and

Burlington, VT

THE VERMONT TOWN MEETING

A Vermont tradition that began in colonial times continues today as the dominant form of local government. It is the town meeting. A town meeting allows every citizen to participate in decisions that will affect their lives. The towns and cities in Vermont today continue as the major local government units, with the counties serving mainly as state law-enforcement and judicial districts. However, while the small towns continue to have the old-fashioned town meetings, many larger towns and cities have found it too awkward a way to do business. Many have followed the lead of Brattleboro, which in 1961 started a different form of the town meeting, one at which business was conducted by selected representatives. Even today, Town Meeting Day is celebrated throughout the state every year on the first Tuesday in March.

Sap gathering

soon became popular vacation resorts.

There were more tough economic times in the early 1990s, though the tourism industry has continued to have a strong presence. The state, however, has enacted strict environmental protection laws, which sometimes come in conflict with the growing numbers of vacationers, as well as those living in other states who look to the Green Mountain State for a second home. After all, Vermont still has much of a small, rural setting that reminds people of quieter times. With more people coming to the state to live and to visit, it may become more difficult to enforce the laws that serve to uphold Vermont's rural character.

Other Things to Know About Vermont

- In 1777, Vermont passed the first constitution to prohibit slavery and allow all men to vote.
- The first ski tow in the United States was established in Vermont in 1934.
- The name *Vermont* is derived from the French words *vert*, meaning "green," and *mont*, meaning "mountain." Not surprisingly, it is known as The Green Mountain State.
- Forest still covers about three-quarters of all the land in Vermont.
- The University of Vermont and State Agricultural College at Burlington were chartered in 1791.
- Though no battles were fought in Vermont during the Civil War, a band of Confederates operating out of Canada in October 1864, crossed the border into Saint Albans, Vermont, and robbed the town's banks of $200,000. It was considered the northernmost action of the war.

NATURAL RESOURCES: wood, beef cattle, hay, apples, cheese, eggs, maple sugar and syrup, milk, sand and gravel, stone, granite, slate, and talc

MANUFACTURED PRODUCTS: lumber, machinery, electric and electronic equipment, processed food, printed materials, measuring instruments, and metal, wood, and paper products

WILDLIFE: white-tailed deer, bear, moose, bobcat, muskrat, mink, raccoon, landlocked salmon, trout, northern pike, walleyed pike, ruffed grouse, ring-necked pheasant, turkey, ducks, and a variety of small birds

THE IMPORTANCE OF EDUCATION

Education has always been a primary concern for the citizens of Vermont. With the passage of the original state constitution in 1777, Vermont became the first state to establish a clear plan for an educational system beginning at the primary school level and extending through university studies. The first school law was passed in 1782, and provisions for statewide taxation to support free public schools were enacted in 1826. The first academy in the state was founded at Bennington in 1780, and public high schools were established very quickly after 1840. Vermont was also the site of the first "normal school" (an institution for training teachers) in the United States. It was founded at Concord Corner in 1823. In the mid-1990s, Vermont's public schools had one teacher for every fourteen students, a smaller class size than any state except New Jersey.

State flower: Dogwood flower

VIRGINIA

State bird: Cardinal

The first colony to be permanently settled by Europeans, Virginia has a history as old as the country itself. In fact, it might be said that Virginia was one of the most influential states in the nation's years of development. The British surrendered to the Americans at Yorktown, Virginia (effectively ending the Revolutionary War [1775–83]), four of the first five presidents were from Virginia, and many battles of the Civil War (1861–65) were fought in the state. Since those early days, four additional presidents have been born in the Old Dominion State.

It is not surprising that Virginia, set on the eastern seaboard, was chosen as the first place in North America to colonize. That happened in 1607, the year after King James I of England granted the right to colonize Virginia to two commercial companies. After a four-month voyage on three ships, the first colonists sailed into an inlet of Chesapeake Bay. They called their settlement Jamestown. Because the settlement was begun with the idea of tapping the huge supply of natural resources as potential profit for Great Britain, supplies and new colonists were constantly sent over from England and the colony survived. It wasn't until 1614, however, when men were permitted to farm for their own profit, that the colony was revitalized and began to grow. Tobacco was the main crop and gave the settlers a sure source of wealth. By 1624, Virginia had become a royal colony, and it seemed to be there to stay.

By the mid-1640s, most of the Native Americans in the area had been driven westward or had been put on reservations. In 1700, the capital was moved from Jamestown to Williamsburg, and Virginia had become the largest of the English colonies with some 58,000 residents. After the French and Indian War (1754–63) ended, the area continued to prosper, but soon dissatisfaction against England began growing. It was Virginia (along with Massachusetts) that spearheaded the movement against British rule resulting in the American Revolution. Virginians played a major role in America's decision to declare independence, fought bravely in the war, then helped to shape the new country.

On June 25, 1788, Virginia became the tenth state to ratify the Constitution of the United States. During the early decades of the nineteenth century, however, the population of Virginia declined. Constant planting of tobacco had depleted the soil, and farmers sought fertile fields elsewhere.

Slavery would become the major issue leading to the Civil War, with Virginia first rejecting secession, then finally joining the Confederacy after the war began in 1861.

Fifty counties west of the Allegheny Mountains, however, remained loyal to the Union. They eventually formed a separate government, and in June 1863, they seceded from Virginia and began to function as the state of West Virginia.

After many battles on Virginia soil, the South was defeated. Virginia, like the other states in the Confederacy, would see the lifestyle of its residents changed dramatically. The state wasn't readmitted to the Union until January 1870. Reconstruction was difficult. Sharecropping and tenant farming took the place of the great plantations. The state had a huge debt, and many people were steeped in poverty.

In the final two decades of the century, northern capital began spurring the growth of industry in the former farming land. Textile mills and cigarette factories were built in many locations, and the railroads were expanded. New centers of population sprang up in growing cities such as Roanoke, Norfolk, and Newport News. At Newport News, one of the nation's largest shipyards was emerging, and in the mountain counties coal mines and sawmills began turning a profit. The fishing industry in the Chesapeake Bay was also prospering.

The outset of the twentieth century was also good for Virginia. Farm prices were up. World War I (1914–18) provided wartime

The Blue Ridge Mountains

jobs in armament factories. Because Virginia became a center for the production of synthetic fibers, chemicals, and paper products in the 1920s and 1930s, the state was able to recover from the Great Depression faster than most. The expansion of government agencies in nearby Washington, D.C., resulted in the growth of suburban communities and kept billions of federal dollars in the state for construction of military bases and ships. In addition, the tourism industry began to grow in the final decades of the century.

Though Virginia had the same problems as other southern states in the battle for civil rights, it eventually emerged the better for it. In 1989, Virginian L. Douglas Wilder, a Democrat, became the first African

Mount Vernon

Visitors to Virginia can visit the restored homes of George Washington (Mount Vernon); of Thomas Jefferson (Monticello); and of James Monroe (Ashlawn).

VIRGINIANS EVERYWHERE

During America's formative years, citizens from Virginia played amazingly major roles. Virginian Peyton Randolph was the president of the first Continental Congress in September 1774. It was Virginian Patrick Henry who urged many to seek independence from Britain when he said, "Give me liberty or give me death!" At the second Continental Congress, Virginia's Richard Henry Lee first addressed the notion of independence, and Virginian Thomas Jefferson was asked to write the Declaration of Independence. After the Revolution, Virginia delegate James Madison contributed so much to the drafting of the Constitution that he became known as the Father of the Constitution. Virginian John Marshall served as chief justice of the Supreme Court from 1801 to 1835, further strengthening the Constitution. And of the first five U.S. presidents, four were Virginia born.

American to be elected the governor of any state. By 1990, Virginia's per-capita income was above the national average and the highest of any southern state. As with other states, there are still problems that need to be addressed. There is a large disparity between the prosperous suburbs and struggling inner cities. And while new, high-tech businesses have grown, some of the older industries—such as coal mines, tobacco farms, and cigarette factories—have declined. But Virginia has a long history of change and adaptation.

HISTORY MIGHT HAVE CHANGED

Virginia's role in the Confederacy during the Civil War was very apparent. Many battles were fought on its soil, there was devastation wreaked by Union troops, and a difficult Reconstruction period followed. What many people do not know, however, is how close Virginia came to fighting on the Union side. Had that happened, the entire course of the war and of the state might have been changed.

In the years before the war, Virginia simply was not as strongly proslavery and potentially secessionist as the other states in the Deep South. In 1832, there was an act to abolish slavery in the state. It was defeated by a mere seven votes. After Abraham Lincoln won the presidential election of 1860, the southern states began seceding from the Union. Virginia moved to stop the secession. The legislature called for a peace convention in February 1861. But the seven seceding states failed to send a delegate, and the convention was disbanded. Then on April 4, 1861, the Virginia state convention met to vote on secession. It rejected the move by a two-to-one margin. It was only after the attack on Fort Sumter by Confederate troops —which began the Civil War—that Virginia reconsidered. Virginians rejected Abraham Lincoln's call for volunteer troops to put down what was called an insurrection. Not wanting to fight against sister states from the South, the Virginia convention felt it had no choice, and on April 17, 1861, it finally voted to secede and join the Confederacy.

After all, that's where everything began.

Federally maintained Arlington National Cemetery features the Tomb of the Unknown Soldier, the graves of John F. Kennedy and Robert Kennedy, and the graves of soldiers from every American war.

Other Things to Know About Virginia

- There is a restoration of a colonial village at Williamsburg with more than eighty homes, public buildings, and shops that are at least 200 years old.
- The Barter Theater at Abington got its name during the Great Depression of the 1930s, when actors gave performances in exchange for food.
- At Jamestown, there are full-sized copies of the first fort and the ships that the first colonists sailed from England.

NATURAL RESOURCES: tobacco, cotton, beef cattle, chickens, eggs, corn, hogs, milk, peanuts, soybeans, apples, tomatoes, turkeys, wood, bluefish, clams, crabs, oysters, scallops, sea trout, flounder, coal, sand and gravel, iron oxide, trap rock, lime, and vermiculite

MANUFACTURED PRODUCTS: tobacco products, chemicals, electric and electronic equipment, clothing, textiles, furniture and fixtures, lumber and wood products, processed food, machinery, paper products, printing and publishing, and transportation equipment

WILDLIFE: white-tailed deer, black bear, bobcat, red fox, mink, gray fox, beaver, river otter, muskrat, timber rattlesnake, northern copperhead, eastern cottonmouth snake, thirty-two species of nonpoisonous snakes, box turtle, northern fence lizard, wild turkey, bobwhite quail, bald eagle, red-tailed hawk, peregrine falcon, osprey, migrating birds, shore birds, and several species of whales

State flower: Rhododendron

WASHINGTON

State bird: Willow goldfinch

Located in the northernmost corner of the Pacific Northwest, the state of Washington is still characterized as a place of unspoiled beauty. There are magnificent glacial mountains, dense forests, pristine lakes and streams, and acres upon acres of golden grain. The city of Seattle is the most important city in the Pacific Northwest; its large port is the gateway to both East Asia and the Arctic North. The Columbia River, which runs through the central part of the state, has often been called the state's most important resource. Washington is the only state named after an American president.

The state has two different climatic regions. West of the Cascade Mountain range, the area is exposed to rain-bearing winds from the Pacific throughout the year, bringing it mild but wet winters and cool summers. East of the Cascades, it is much drier, with hotter summers and colder winters. Several of the mountain peaks in Washington are well known. Mount Rainier is the highest, rising to 14,410 feet; it often presents a dangerous challenge to mountain climbers. Mount Saint Helens is still remembered for a violent volcanic eruption in 1980 that took many lives and caused extensive damage. Yet Washington is a thriving state with a solid economy and burgeoning tourist trade. For many, it's a great place to live, and for others a great place to visit.

Due to its location, Washington was not settled early. It was the Lewis and Clark Expedition of 1804 and 1805, which included the exploration of the Columbia River to the Pacific coast, that really sparked the interest of fur traders. Soon, several companies were operating in the area, making a profit by trapping, selling, and trading furs.

Other pioneers began streaming west once the Oregon Trail opened in 1843. Many settled in the Oregon country, which included present-day Washington. The Oregon Territory was officially created in 1848. At first, most settlers went to the Willamette Valley in Oregon. But after 1848, many headed north into Washington to start settlements there. Again there was conflict with Native Americans. Washington saw a great deal of bloodshed between 1855 and 1859, but after that, most Native Americans were moved to reservations.

Settlers began planting wheat and vegetables. They gathered berries, fished for salmon and halibut, and killed wild game. There was an abundance of lumber, used to build houses and furniture. Industry began springing up on the western side of the state, while agriculture thrived on the eastern half.

145

Once the railroad arrived in 1875, the area became even more populated. With the transcontinental railroad in place, the population grew from about 75,000 in 1880 to 357,000 in 1890. The prospect of jobs working for the railroad attracted many African American and Asian people.

The Washington legislature first petitioned for statehood in 1878, but at that time it was felt the Washington Territory was too large. Finally, on November 11, 1889—with the boundaries settled—Washington became the nation's forty-second state. Seven years later, in 1896, gold was discovered in Alaska, and that also proved a boon to Washington. Merchants in Seattle sold gear and food to prospectors. At the same time, trade with Alaska and East Asia spurred the shipbuilding industry. The turn of the twentieth century also saw the timber, fish, and mineral industries prospering.

Industry continued to grow during World War I (1914–18), especially shipbuilding and fishing. The Great Depression of the 1930s saw an economic slowdown, but in 1933, the Works Progress Administration

Seattle is Washington's largest city, with more than a half million people. However, the capital, Olympia, has barely 40,000 residents.

(WPA) began construction of the Grand Coulee Dam across the Columbia River. When completed in 1942, it was the largest dam ever built at that time and began generating huge amounts of electricity to the region. Another WPA dam—the Bonneville Dam—began providing power even earlier, in 1937.

During World War II (1939–45), there was a huge demand for ships and aircraft. New plants were built to supplement existing ones. The aluminum industry began operating in 1940, while the Hanford atomic installation opened at Richland in 1943. All that gave Washington the second highest number of defense contracts in the country. Once again, the population surged. In the 1960s and 1970s, Washingtonians began to be concerned about the natural beauty and resources of their state. More environmental laws were passed. It took ten years, for instance, to make Lake Washington pure enough for swimming and fish preservation. Other regulations were passed to help keep

THE COLUMBIA RIVER, AN ELECTRICAL BONANZA

The Columbia has probably contributed as much or more to the economy and well-being of a state than any other river in the country. In the early days, it was a source of food, water, and commerce. Then, in 1933, construction began on the Grand Coulee Dam on the river. Today, the dam's hydro-electricity-generating capacity totals nearly 6,500 megawatts, which makes it one of the world's greatest hydroelectric installations. With several other dams on the river, the waters of the Columbia provide inexpensive electric power for industry—and irrigation for agriculture on the dry eastern side of the Cascade Range. Nevertheless, some scientists believe that the Columbia River is environmentally threatened and that action should be taken to reverse the changes made to it.

the air and water clean. The theme of the 1974 World's Fair at Spokane was "Progress without Pollution."

The late 1980s and early 1990s brought new jobs, as high-tech companies began opening in Seattle and other cities. Once again, the population grew, as more newcomers arrived in the state. In fact, according to the 1990 census, more than half the residents of metropolitan Seattle were born outside Washington. Then again, since the beginning, Washington has constantly beckoned people from other areas. It retains that kind of attraction to the present day.

MOUNT SAINT HELENS BLOWS ITS TOP

Mount Saint Helens, located in the Cascade Range in southwestern Washington, was a picturesque peak stretching some 9,677 feet toward the sky. Like other mountains in the range, it was actually a dormant volcano. In fact, Mount Saint Helens had been dormant since 1857, and people had long stopped worrying about it. But in early 1980, the volcano showed signs of coming to life. Volcanic activity kept increasing until the morning of May 18, 1980, when it erupted with more violence than any volcano in the history of the continental United States. The top of the mountain literally blew off, spewing a cloud of gases and ash twelve miles in the air. All life in an area of some seventy square miles was destroyed. The volcanic ash was carried hundreds of miles by the wind. When it all cleared, Mount Saint Helens was some 1,300 feet shorter than it had been before the blast.

Mount Rainier

Other Things to Know About Washington

- Fort Vancouver National Historic Site is a restored 1825 fur-trading post opened to the public.
- Washington produces more apples, pears, and sweet cherries than any other state.
- Washington ranks second only to Oregon in the production of lumber.
- During the Great Depression of the 1930s, folksinger Woody Guthrie was sent to Washington by the federal government to write songs about the construction of the Grand Coulee Dam. One of his famous songs was "Roll on, Columbia."
- When he was elected governor of Washington in 1997, Gary Locke became the first Asian American governor in the continental United States.

NATURAL RESOURCES: chickens, beef cattle, eggs, wheat, hay, potatoes, fruit, hops, milk, wood, clams, crab, halibut, oysters, salmon, sea urchins, shrimp, rockfish, whiting, clay, sand and gravel, stone, coal, gold, and diatomite

MANUFACTURED PRODUCTS: lumber, processed food, clothing, electric and electronic equipment, machinery, printing materials, passenger planes, aluminum, and metal, wood, and paper products

WILDLIFE: Olympic elk, white-tailed deer, mule deer, black bear, mountain goat, cougar, Canada lynx, coyote, red fox, otter, prairie rattlesnake, a variety of reptiles and amphibians, a variety of small birds, bald eagle, hawk, owl, a variety of waterfowl and seabirds, killer whale, harbor seal, five species of salmon, steelhead (a seagoing rainbow trout), large- and smallmouth black bass, white sturgeon, tuna, albacore, smelt, halibut, and clams and oysters

State flower: Rhododendron

WEST VIRGINIA

State bird: Cardinal

West Virginia is a unique state. First, it is the only state that was formed by breaking away from another state over ideological differences. It is also a state where the most valuable natural resource—coal—has proved both a positive and a negative for the land and the environment. Located in the eastern United States in the heart of the Appalachian Highlands, West Virginia has mostly mountainous terrain and a picturesque landscape. The state has irregular boundaries, formed largely by rivers and mountains. Some say it looks like a large pan with two handles, one in the north and the other in the east. For that reason, it is sometimes called the Panhandle State.

Virginia was the site of the first colony in America, settled at Jamestown in 1607. Though the colony's charter, drawn in 1609, left its boundaries to the west open, it was the mountain ranges—the Blue Ridge and, to the west, the Alleghenies—that created a barrier to expansion, and not a single effort to cross them was made for years.

The first real exploration beyond the mountains occurred in 1716. Settlement in the fertile valleys followed around 1730 and continued slowly for the next quarter century. By the time of the American Revolution (1775–83), settlement had started accelerating. In 1800, there were some 78,000 people in the area that would become West Virginia, with most of the settlers taking up farming and the raising of livestock. Over the next several decades, the area would continue to grow because of the

natural resources that were in abundance—namely timber, salt, iron, coal, gas, and oil. In order to use these resources, it became necessary for the area to become industrialized.

The first major industry was salt making. Iron smelting followed. The value of coal wasn't realized until saltmakers began using it in 1817 to fire their furnaces. By 1841, natural gas was used in industry for the first time, and digging for oil came in 1859.

During these years, people in the Western Counties forged a lifestyle different than that of eastern Virginia. They didn't need slaves because there were no big plantations, and many of the residents openly opposed the idea. The beginning of the Civil War (1861–65) brought the conflict to a head. In October 1861, the Western Counties voted to form a new state. They drew up a constitution, and on June 20, 1863, West Virginia was officially severed from Virginia and became the thirty-fifth state of the Union.

After the war, and in the final decades of the nineteenth century, West Virginia continued its industrial revolution. Locks and dams were built on the rivers, while rails were laid in every part of the state. Steam power took the place of waterpower in the sawmills in 1881, and by 1909 the state was the largest producer of lumber in the country. Coal and oil production were also growing, as was the production of natural gas.

By the start of World War I in 1914, West Virginia employed more than 70,000 workers in manufacturing. Most of the industry involved extracting coal, salt, iron ore, oil, and natural gas. During the war, chemical plants sprang up, creating more jobs, and plants were built to manufacture compounds to make rubber, plastics, and antifreeze. It was a total industrialization of a former farming state.

After the war, labor-management problems began. The miners tried to unionize, and there was much violence throughout the 1920s. In 1920, for example, some 50,000 West Virginians belonged to the United Mine Workers of America (UMWA). The miners, however, lost many of their battles and, by 1932, membership in the UMWA had dwindled to a few hundred.

The Great Depression of the 1930s ended the coal boom and led to hard times for the state. New industries and a back-to-the-farm movement helped, and when World War II (1939–45) created a demand for coal, production mounted once again. The steel industry also continued to grow. But in the years following the war, increasing mechanization of coal mining put many miners out of work. So many people left that ghost towns were created, and the population in the cities began to decline. New methods of strip mining also began to devastate the countryside and create environmental problems for both humans and wildlife.

There was more economic depression from the 1970s to the 1990s. Finally, West Virginians began realizing that because so much of their natural resources had been mined, their environment and heritage had been compromised. Piles of worked-out drift-mine waste known as "gob dumps" dotted the landscape. The waste products often burned though spontaneous combustion, igniting forest fires and polluting the air. The state also accepted waste disposal brought in from other states. Stronger environmental laws were finally demanded.

THE RAID AT HARPERS FERRY

One event that led the South closer to secession prior to the Civil War also served as motivation for the Western Counties to become a separate state. It happened in 1859 at Harpers Ferry, a town in eastern West Virginia where a U.S. armory had been built that housed many weapons. A man named John Brown—who felt slavery should be abolished—brought his men to Harpers Ferry. He wanted to establish an independent free state in the Virginia mountains that would serve as a haven for runaway slaves. Brown and twenty-one men captured the armory. But before they could leave with the weapons, they were surrounded by a detachment of U.S. Marines under the command of Colonel Robert E. Lee. Brown was captured and later tried for treason and murder. He was subsequently executed, but his daring raid attracted national attention and helped divide the country into pro- and antislavery factions.

Today, much has to be done to reclaim the natural beauty of West Virginia. The economy is still based mainly on manufacturing and mining, and the state is one of the poorer in the country. Jobs in service areas and wholesale and retail trade have grown. Numerous computer software companies have also located in the state. Toyota Motor Corporation is now producing engines there, and the Federal Bureau of Investigation Fingerprint Center is a major employer at Clarksburg. Progress has been slow, but West Virginia continues to make strides as it changes with the times.

Highland Scenic Highway

Visitors to the Cass Scenic Railroad can ride on steam-driven locomotives.

Other Things to Know About West Virginia

- West Virginia ships more coal overseas than any other state.
- West Virginia is the second least urbanized state, behind Vermont. Only 36 percent of its inhabitants are classified as urban. The rest are rural.
- Jackson's Mill, near Weston, features the boyhood home of famed Confederate general Stonewall Jackson.
- There were so many raids within the state during the Civil War that the town of Romney changed hands fifty-six times.
- The need for better control of mining methods was never more apparent than at Buffalo Creek in Logan County in 1972. A mine waste dam that held back 30 million gallons of water burst without warning, sending a thirty-foot-high wave through the valley: it wiped out sixteen small communities and left 125 people dead.

NATURAL RESOURCES: corn, chickens, sheep, wool, fruit, milk, coal, natural gas, petroleum, sand and gravel, and stone

MANUFACTURED PRODUCTS: automobile parts, chemicals, lumber, machinery, clothing, printing, and metal, wood, stone, clay, and glass products

WILDLIFE: deer, black bear, beaver, otter, mink, bobcat, fox, groundhog, opossum, timber rattlesnake, copperhead snake, turkey vulture, hawk, owl, eagle, falcon, osprey, migratory grebe, loon, ducks and geese, trout, bass, and pike

State flower: Wood violet

WISCONSIN

State bird: Robin

Wisconsin is located in the north central United States and is loaded with lakes. In addition to being bordered by two of the Great Lakes, there are some 9,000 smaller lakes within the state. The majority of the state, however, is covered by rolling plains that have always been fertile planting ground, producing wheat and fodder for the dairy industry. Though dairy products—especially cheese—still play a large part in Wisconsin's economy, the state has long diversified, with most of its heavy industry located around the city of Milwaukee and other cities along the shores of Lake Michigan.

Like other northern states, Wisconsin has long and cold winters with short, fairly hot summers. Thunderstorms—sometimes spawning dangerous tornadoes—are not uncommon in the spring and summer. Once covered extensively by forest, Wisconsin still has some 42 percent of its land heavily forested.

Wisconsin's early history is similar to other states in the area. French explorers came first, toward the middle of the seventeenth century. They found a forested land inhabited by various Native American groups and rich in fur-bearing animals. Soon trappers and traders from Canada began arriving, with the first trading post built at La Baye (now Green Bay) in 1684. For the next eighty years, the area was mainly used by trappers. The French and English domination of the area ended with the

American Revolution (1775–83), when Britain ceded all territory east of the Mississippi River to the United States. The region was then incorporated into the Northwest Territory, which was created in 1787.

It wasn't until the War of 1812 ended in 1815 that settlement of Wisconsin really began. The army built several forts in the area, and small settlements began springing up around them. In the 1820s, the first real rush of settlers came. Many arrived because of a lead-mining boom. By 1840, the Wisconsin region was producing nearly half of the total U.S. output of lead ore.

Large numbers of European immigrants began coming in search of work, and by 1850, the population had grown to about 305,000 people, with more than one-third of the residents foreign born. Many took up farming, and by the 1840s, the wheat crop in the Wisconsin area was the second largest in the nation. During this period of heavy immigration, the clamoring for statehood began.

One reason was that the people needed government aid to improve roads, railroads, canals, and harbors. The economy was expanding faster than the means to exploit it. In May 1848, Wisconsin became the nation's thirtieth state. Its northern location made it staunchly antislavery, and many residents fought on the Union side during the Civil War (1861–65). After the war, the state began to change and develop as it headed toward the twentieth century.

Rail lines increased everywhere. Lumbering became a major industry. Dairy farming replaced wheat as the chief agricultural product, and the state began producing large amounts of cheese. The meatpacking and tanning industries were natural by-products of livestock raising. Milwaukee began to flourish as a metalworking center and as a manufacturer of farming, dairying, and milling machinery.

In the first decade of the twentieth century, Wisconsin governor Robert La Follette pushed for the passage of some landmark reform laws. Anticorruption and civil service measures were passed, as was a law for direct primary elections that gave voters a larger say and took power from the political bosses. Railroads came under state regulation, and laws were passed to help farmers form cooperatives to maximize their profits. La Follette was a breath of fresh air in an era when corruption in politics and labor affected much of the country.

The state prospered again during World War I (1914–18). However, more difficult times began in 1920. Wisconsin had many breweries that produced beer, and this industry was hurt by Prohibition (the national ban on alcohol that began in 1920 and lasted until 1933). By the early 1930s, there was a national depression that hit Wisconsin hard. Many were out of work, and it took World War II (1939–45) to jump-start the state's economy. Manufacturing grew and continued to prosper in the 1950s and 1960s, as agriculture also made a comeback. However, both the dairy and manufacturing industries suffered from mechanization that affected the number of farms and jobs available.

At the outset of the new millennium, the economy was again stabilizing. The dairy

Packers' fans are called cheeseheads.

TITLETOWN, U.S.A.

Most professional sports franchises today are located in large cities, where there are enough fans to fill huge stadiums and people to support the rising costs and players' salaries. In the early days of the National Football League, when many teams were in small cities, a new franchise began in Green Bay, Wisconsin. The team was called the Packers because the owner of a meatpacking plant bought the uniforms. While other small-town teams have long disappeared, the Green Bay Packers remain one of the NFLs flagship franchises. Although the team had success in the early days of the league, its reputation was really made in the 1960s, when a tough taskmaster named Vince Lombardi became the coach. From 1961 to 1967, the Packers won five NFL championships in seven years. They also won the first two Super Bowls ever played. Lombardi and the Packers players from that era became so legendary that the city of Green Bay became known as Titletown, U.S.A.

Dairy farm

industry continues to produce a large percentage of the nation's butter and cheese, and farmland continues to cover nearly half of the state's land area, while manufacturing provides the largest share of Wisconsin's income.

Tourism has also increased, as people take advantage of Wisconsin's natural beauty. Hiking, camping, swimming, boating, golfing, hunting, and fishing are all popular summertime activities, while skating, skiing, snowmobiling, and tobogganing are popular in the winter.

NATIVE AMERICAN COMEBACK

As more white settlers began flocking to Wisconsin by the 1830s and 1840s, most Native American groups were forced to leave the state. Several groups remained, living on reservations established in the northern part of the state. Those living on reservations were for the most part very poor, struggling with unemployment throughout most of the twentieth century. It wasn't until the 1980s and 1990s that the Wisconsin Ojibwa group asserted rights, under nineteenth-century treaties, to hunt and spear fish on traditional lands off the reservations. When the courts upheld these rights, there was some violent reaction from whites. Then, in 1987, the Wisconsin Constitution was amended to allow for a state lottery and other gambling avenues, and Native Americans began to operate casinos. Those around Milwaukee, Green Bay, and Wisconsin Dells, have been very profitable. The casinos have brought jobs and money for education, health, and cultural programs to some of the Native Americans.

Other Things to Know About Wisconsin

- The Ringling Brothers gave their first show in Wisconsin in 1882, the first step in developing their famous circus.
- The first kindergarten in American was opened in Wisconsin in 1865.
- The state name was taken from the Wisconsin River. That term was derived from the French version of an Ojibwa term that may mean either "gathering of the waters" or "place of the beaver." The French spelling was *Ouisconsin*.
- At the time of the Civil War, many foreign-born immigrants were living in Wisconsin. Many had left Europe to escape war, and when they heard the Union was going to draft troops in 1862, antidraft riots broke out in several cities. Fortunately, there were enough volunteers to fill the quota.
- Wisconsin suffered a great natural disaster in October 1871, when a forest fire swept through several northeastern counties. It killed more than 1,000 people and caused $5 million worth of damage. Coincidentally, the fire began the same night as the Great Chicago Fire.
- Wisconsin resident Victor Louis Berger became the first Socialist Party candidate elected to Congress in 1910.
- In 1932, the Wisconsin legislature passed the nation's first unemployment compensation law, which served as a model for laws later passed in other states and by the federal government.

NATURAL RESOURCES: milk, corn, eggs, hay, wood, potatoes, mink, cranberries, vegetables, buffalo fish, catfish, whitefish, mussels, herring, chub, sand and gravel, and stone

MANUFACTURED PRODUCTS: cheese and butter, ice cream, dried milk, beer, canned vegetables, meat products, electric and electronic equipment, lumber, processed food, machinery, transportation equipment, printed materials, and metal, plastic, wood, and paper products

WILDLIFE: black bear, timber wolf, Canada lynx, elk, white-tailed deer, muskrat, red and gray fox, coyote, mink, otter, beaver, porcupine, migratory birds, ring-necked pheasant, Hungarian partridge, sharp-tailed grouse, ruffed grouse, bobwhite, hawks and owls, wild turkey, bald eagle, songbirds, muskellunge, northern pike, walleye, large- and smallmouth bass, lake trout, and crappie

State flower: Indian paintbrush

WYOMING

State bird: Meadowlark

Though it is the ninth largest in area, Wyoming is the least populated state in the Union. It is also the fiftieth state in manufacturing. But not everyone complains about the small population or lack of industry. Wyoming is a western state of great natural beauty, a place where the unspoiled Yellowstone National Park is visited by thousands of tourists each year. The capital (and largest city) of Cheyenne has just over 50,000 residents. The wide open spaces are still there in abundance.

Surrounded by Montana, South Dakota, Nebraska, Colorado, Utah, and Idaho, Wyoming is part of a group of states that were among the last settled by whites in the country. Trappers and mountain men came to seek their fortunes in the 1830s. In 1834, a fort was built on the Laramie River as a meeting place for Native Americans and trappers to trade, and as a stopping point for westward travelers. It was the first real settlement of any kind in Wyoming.

During the 1840s, thousands of immigrants began passing through Wyoming on their way to Oregon and California. It is estimated that from 1841 to 1868, between 350,000 and 400,000 people passed over the land. Very few stayed. Fighting began between Native Americans and the immigrants, which continued until 1876, when the Sioux defeated General George Custer at the Little Big Horn River in Montana. Additional federal troops were called in, and

by the spring of 1877, almost all Native Americans in Wyoming had been moved to reservations.

By then, more whites were coming to Wyoming. The population grew from less than 1,000 in the mid-1860s, to 11,000 in 1868. A year earlier, gold was discovered at South Pass, and construction of the Union Pacific Railroad reached Wyoming. That opened up more opportunities, and coal mines were soon built along the rail line. Makeshift towns soon appeared along the tracks, and in 1868, the Wyoming Territory was created out of parts of the Dakota, Utah, and Idaho Territories. The area was finally getting an identity of its own.

The completion of the rail lines also encouraged cattle ranching in the territory. Soon hundreds of cattle ranchers were driving their herds from Texas to Wyoming so they could winter on public lands before being shipped to market. By the middle of

Old Faithful

THE BEAUTY OF YELLOWSTONE PARK

In 1872, President Ulysses S. Grant signed a bill making Yellowstone Park the world's first national park. Today, it is still one of America's most beautiful natural wonders. Located almost entirely in the northwestern corner of Wyoming, Yellowstone is a broad volcanic plateau surrounded by mountain ranges. It is known for its spectacular geysers, hot springs, canyons, and fossil forests. The most famous geyser, Old Faithful, erupts on average every seventy-five minutes, shooting a column of steam and hot water some 184 feet in the air for about five minutes. Between 10,000 and 12,000 gallons of water are expelled at each eruption. Yellowstone is also one of the largest wildlife sanctuaries in the country, with more than 300 animal species found there. In August and September 1988, a series of fires—fueled by dry and windy summer weather—burned more than 35 percent of the park.

the 1880s, there were an estimated one million head of cattle grazing on the rich grass. The result was overgrazing, and the industry soon suffered. Sheep were also introduced to the area, angering some cattle ranchers. The two groups rarely got along, and their animosity sometimes erupted into violence.

With mining and ranching growing, the clamor for statehood began. Wyoming voters tried in 1889, but there was some opposition in the U.S. Congress, opponents claiming the territory's population was too small to merit statehood. The objection did not last long. On July 10, 1890, Wyoming became the forty-fourth state of the Union, with the largest city, Cheyenne, its capital.

There were still many traces of the old Wild West. Cattle rustling and frontier justice were not uncommon right up to the turn of the century. Chinese immigrants brought in to work on the railroad came in conflict with European immigrants, another kind of animosity that erupted in violence. But workers were needed. By 1903, the coal industry was so widespread that one-tenth of the state's workers were miners.

The oil industry also developed at the turn of the century. The first refinery was built at Casper in 1894, and oilfields sprang up at a number of other locations during the first decades of the twentieth century. Irrigation projects also spurred agriculture, as dams were built on many of the state's waterways. For the first two decades of the twentieth century, agriculture increased and more homesteaders came into the state. The Great Depression of the 1930s stopped much of this progress, but World War II (1939–45) led both agriculture and mining to take an upturn.

After the war, mineral production surpassed ranching and farming as the state's most important industry. In the 1950s, uranium deposits were discovered in various locations throughout the state, and while coal declined, petroleum resources boomed in the 1950s and 1960s. That pattern of ups and downs in those same few industries has continued right up to the present day.

Efforts to diversify the economy have not always met with success. Many natives of the state prefer that Wyoming remain sparsely populated and free of industry. Wyoming's natural beauty has become attractive to tourists, who flock to both Yellowstone and Grand Teton National Parks. Hiking, skiing, and mountain climbing are popular activities. Because of the increase in tourism, environmental measures must be closely observed to preserve the natural beauty of the land, which for the most part still resembles the Wyoming of old.

HORSES ON THE WYOMING PLAINS

Before the mid-seventeenth century, Native American groups living on the Plains in the Wyoming area moved around on foot. To hunt bison, they would build corrals made of brush and poles near steep bluffs or ravines. They would then drive the herds toward the corral, and when the bison entered, men hiding behind the walls chased them over the cliffs. The men then could simply gather the meat and hides. But by the middle of the century, horses were introduced to the area, giving Native Americans better mobility. Now they could carry more goods as well as transport their young and old much more easily. And they could drive bison over cliffs without building corrals.

Other Things to Know About Wyoming

- Wyoming was the first place to specifically give women the right to vote. The territory did this in 1869 and retained the policy when it entered the Union in 1890.
- The federal government owns almost half the land in Wyoming.
- Wyoming ranks first in coal production among all the states.
- Wyoming has only five cities with a population of more than 15,000 people.
- When explorer John Frémont first saw the mountains of Wyoming in 1842, he wrote it seemed as if "Nature had collected all her beauties together in one chosen place."
- Before the creation of the Wyoming Territory in 1868, Wyoming was part of the Oregon Territory (1848), the Washington Territory (1853), the Dakota Territory (1861), the Idaho Territory (1863), the Montana Territory (1864), and (again) the Dakota Territory (1864).
- During the 1920s, there were ninety-nine bank failures in Wyoming, mainly due to drought and declining farm prices. Of the 133 banks operating in the state in 1920, only thirty-four remained ten years later.

NATURAL RESOURCES: beef cattle, buffalo, sheep, wool, wheat, barley, corn, sugar beets, dry beans, hay, wood, coal, natural gas, petroleum, and bentonite

MANUFACTURED PRODUCTS: petroleum, lumber, chemicals, printed materials, and coal, wood, stone, clay, and glass products

WILDLIFE: moose, elk, pronghorn, antelope, bighorn sheep, mule deer, grizzly bear, mountain lion, wolf, fox, mink, coyote, bobcat, prairie rattlesnake, sage grouse, wild turkey, ring-necked pheasant, a variety of hawks and owls, bald eagle, golden eagle, osprey, trumpeter swan, white pelican, great blue heron, California gull, rainbow trout, bass, walleye, and channel catfish

Index